Hugh Hood

Twayne's World Authors Series

Canadian Literature

Robert Lecker, Editor

McGill University

TWAS 709

HUGH HOOD
(1928–   )
Photograph by Sam Tata

Hugh Hood

By Keith Garebian

Twayne Publishers • Boston

Hugh Hood

Keith Garebian

Copyright © 1983 by G. K. Hall & Company
All Rights Reserved
Published by Twayne Publishers
A Division of G. K. Hall & Company
70 Lincoln Street
Boston, Massachusetts 02111

Book Production by John Amburg

Book Design by Barbara Anderson

Printed on permanent/durable acid-free
paper and bound in the United States of
America

Library of Congress Cataloging in Publication Data

Garebian, Keith.
  Hugh Hood.

  (Twayne's world authors series ; TWAS 709)
  Bibliography: p. 142
  Includes index.
  1. Hood, Hugh—Criticism and interpretation.
I. Title. II. Series.
PR9199.3.H59Z68   1983   813'.54   83-10683
ISBN 0-8057-6556-5

Contents

About the Author

Keith Garebian is a teacher and freelance writer who lives in Toronto. He has published poetry, features, interviews, scholarly articles, and reviews in over forty newspapers, journals, and anthologies.

He holds a doctorate in Canadian and Commonwealth Literature, and has taught courses at the Thomas More Institute for Adult Education, Dawson College, McGill University, and Concordia University.

A member of the first Board of Directors for the Canadian Theatre Critics Association, he was runner-up in 1982 for the Nathan Cohen Award for Outstanding Theatre Criticism in Canada.

Preface

Were Hugh Hood's fiction only the marvelous documentaries of reality that they were for a long time described as being, this book would not be necessary or justified. If his books contained nothing more than what is to be found in conventional realism, they would not sustain or deserve the rigors of textual criticism. But year after year increases the number of Hood's admirers whose interest is often distinguished by an intensity that borders on religious fervor. Such passionate admiration is not altogether an extravagance, however, because Hood's fiction is Christian allegory beautifully assimilated by realism.

Allegory is, at the best of times, a difficult issue for criticism because it nudges the critic into thematic description and urges him to treat even the most delicate artistic expressions of ideas as historical documents. But allegory, in a sense, is what all criticism tends toward, for, as Northrop Frye has shown, commentary is allegorization insofar as it is "an attaching of ideas to the structure of poetic imagery."[1]

Now while it has been generally agreed by critics in Canada that Hugh Hood writes good fiction (particularly in his short stories), the eddies of argument and persuasion have not usually, in their wild whirl, shown Hood's true design. It has often been his fate to be praised fulsomely for the tritest or most banal reason, or to be condemned occasionally for digressing eloquently into a mode that is really one of his proper motives for fiction. Everybody who has read Hood's work sees that his sensibility is Christian, but few critics have honored him for his expertise in crafting a fiction (especially in his New Age series) that, in addition to describing phenomena in awesome detail and providing a history of ideas in Canada, manifests in striking degree how literature is a secular analogy for Scripture.

This book attempts to explore Hood's allegorical view of reality. In it I seek to probe the form and scope of the fiction, limiting my analysis of Hood's literary journalism because this genre, despite its interesting interplay with his fiction, is not quantitatively large enough to warrant an entire chapter in itself. I trust my comments will place his journalism in a proper perspective, without either magnifying or reducing its importance.

For obvious reasons this book is an interim report. Hood is a prolific writer whose current project in fiction—a *roman fleuve* in twelve volumes—is a most ambitious one that, by design, will not be completed until the end of this century. The millennium will demand revisions or augmentations in my book, but in the meantime it goes forth. Good sense and celebration, I trust, are its chief spirit; textual scrutiny its main process; and humble suasion the respect it pays its subject.

The book has been completed with the generous help of several people. Hugh Hood himself has always offered the most courteous advice without any expectation that his benevolence might be reciprocated. I thank him for the numerous discussions he has offered me, for the archival material he opened to me, and for his kind permission to quote so freely from his works.

I wish to thank Robert Lecker and Jack David of ECW Press for permission to quote from Hood's books and from an article I prepared on Hood for their series Canadian Writers and Their Works. I thank also Michael Macklem and Oberon Press for permission to quote from *Reservoir Ravine*.

Keith Garebian

Chronology

1928   Born 30 April in Toronto. Educated in parish and high schools.

1955   Ph.D. from the University of Toronto. Thesis on "Theories of Imagination in English Thinkers 1650–1790."

1955–1961   Taught English at St. Joseph College, West Hartford, Connecticut.

1957   Married the painter and theatrical designer Noreen Mallory.

1958   First publication, "The Isolation Booth," in the *Tamarack Review*, no. 9 (Autumn 1958).

1961   Moved to Montreal to teach English Literature at L'Université de Montréal.

1962   *Flying a Red Kite.*

1963   *Flying a Red Kite* awarded the Women's Canadian Club of Toronto literary award. "The End of It" awarded the President's Medal, University of Western Ontario, in 1963 for the short-story category.

1964   *White Figure, White Ground.*

1965   *White Figure, White Ground* awarded the Beta Sigma Phi Award for the best first novel by a Canadian.

1967   *Around the Mountain: Scenes from Montreal Life* and *The Camera Always Lies.*

1968   "It's A Small World" awarded the President's Medal, University of Western Ontario, for the general-article category.

1968–1969   Awarded Canada Council Short Term Grant.

1970   *A Game of Touch,* and a sports biography, *Strength down Centre: The Jean Béliveau Story.* The latter given French translation by Louis Rémillard.

1970–1971   Won Canada Council Senior Arts Award.

1971   *The Fruit Man, The Meat Man & The Manager.*

1972 *You Cant Get There From Here.*

1973 *The Governor's Bridge Is Closed.*

1974 Shared with Alice Munro the Province of Ontario Council for the Arts Award.

1974–1975 Awarded Canada Council Senior Arts Grant.

1975 Published *The Swing in the Garden.* Won the City of Toronto 1975 Book Award. Shared award with *Immigrants: A Portrait of the Urban Experience, 1890–1930,* by Robert F. Harney and Harold Troper.

1976 *Dark Glasses.*

1977 *A New Athens.*

1977–1978 Awarded Canada Council Senior Arts Grant.

1978 *Selected Stories.*

1979 *Reservoir Ravine.* Wrote text and commentary for *Scoring: Seymour Segal's Art of Hockey.* Attended symposium in his honor in October at Stong College, York University, Ontario.

1980 *None Genuine Without This Signature.*

1982 *Black and White Keys.*

Abbreviations

Chapter One
Background and Ambitions

Hugh John Blagdon Hood was born in Toronto on 30 April 1928 of mixed French and English ancestry. His father's side goes back to the Canadian Maritimes and, beyond this, to England, for his paternal grandfather, although born in Shelburne, Ontario, was descended from a naval family of Bridport, England, and was married to Katherine MacDonald from Antigonish, Nova Scotia. The Hood family in England boasted some famous commanders in the eighteenth century. Admiral Samuel Hood, for instance, fought against the French in Nevis, and several of his descendants have been in the British navy ever since.

On his mother's side, Hugh Hood has roots in French Canada. The Blagdons, his mother's family, came from Lévis, Québec, and they, too, like the Hoods, had connections with the navy. Hood's maternal grandfather, however, was a schoolteacher, and Hood's mother, Marguerite Cécile Blagdon, was born in Toronto after her father moved there in the late nineteenth century. Although there was a small but strong French community in Toronto, Marguérite anglicized her name and obtained her education in English, but Hugh Hood remembers hearing French spoken around his house from his earliest childhood.

Hood's father was a bank-teller in 1915, when the family lived on Summerhill Avenue in North Rosedale. The hierarchical character of Canadian society was expressed in Rosedale, particularly by the entrepreneurs and property-owners, and later in *The Swing in the Garden,* Hood would focus on this point in order to show how his protagonist Matt Goderich, a microcosm of his society, is a child of the servant class that lives on the extreme edge of Rosedale. Hood, of course, was never the same sort of child as Matt, but he did live on the same street, Summerhill, and was always conscious that Chorley Park and the lieutenant governor were down at the end, and that this was a vice-regal society. Once as a youth he went to the house of a rich acquaintance of his, a college girl who lived in Forest Hill in a big house. He was greeted at the door by a butler who said, "Miss Anna

I

is in the drawing-room with the other young people, sir." Books had
not taught Hood an effective response: "Should I have greeted him
with an oath and a kick, a curt nod, a handshake and a friendly grin,
a smooth, 'Thank you, Phipps'? You tell me."[1]

More than social class, however, the thing that really dominated
his boyhood was topography—especially the bridges, ravines, and
waterways of Toronto. The city has real labyrinths which uncoil and
connect all the way across town, and it was possible for a boy to walk
from one corner of a street to another locale by descending into one
ravine after another, without coming up to street level. Young Hood
lived in the ravines a large part of his waking hours and dreamed
about them. In fact, the parish school he attended backed onto one,
and ravines have always represented "a permanent range of action" to
him.[2] There was a secret, a mystery, about ravines that darkened his
imagination then and left its mark on it ever since. Hood always
thinks of Toronto as "a city where sooner or later you find yourself
going down into a dark place in the ground" (GB, 9).

Almost as compelling a force on his boyhood imagination were the
bridges, for they, like the ravines, helped to roll up his whole imaginative life into "a ball made up of the primordial fears of falling and
of being entombed, and the human triumph over these fears" (GB,
19). The most obsessive hold on his imagination was exercised by a
bridge near Sherbourne Street, which carried the sign: GOVERNOR'S
BRIDGE CLOSED. The closing of this bridge, as Hood wrote, "is a permanent happening in Toronto" (GB, 15). The powerful joy of recognition which comes out of this continuous closing expresses Hood's
belief in permanence. Unlike Thomas Wolfe, Hood has always found
it possible to go home again—to return to the ravines, bridges, and
underground brooks or lakes that so haunted his boyhood. Opposed
to the Heraclitean notion of flux as the basic cosmic principle, Hood
is always on the side of permanence and continuity (GB, 20). Although rickety, the Governor's Bridge is a permanent emblem of
temptation and peril, and later, when writing of his second home-
place, Quebec, Hood turns his impression of its capital into a symbol
of primeval consolidation by describing the emergence of rock from
the prehistoric deep: "Quebec City is a fortress unlike any other city
on the continent. At the end of the last Ice Age the location was on
an island, as l'Île d'Orléans and Montreal still are. When the waters
had receded enough, just before the dawn of recorded history, a great

natural citadel emerged, towering protectively over the river at the terminal point of deep-water navigation" (*GB,* 84).

Ontario, a vast, paradoxical province with "warm feet and a cool head," probably showed Hood that opposites could be reconciled without necessitating a dualistic conception of reality. From Fort Albany and beyond to the Manitoba border, it is a country of Innuit or Eskimo people. But the Niagara peninsula is warm wine-growing country. As Hood comments: "Eskimos and wine: there's something Hegelian about this province" (*GB,* 61). Evidently the pull of Ontario has never weakened on him, for he spends his summers on Charleston Lake, a few miles north of Brockville (which appears as Stoverville in his New Age series).

Ontario has inspired many Canadian writers, from Sara Jeannette Duncan, Robertson Davies, and Al Purdy to Morley Callaghan, Margaret Atwood, Marian Engel, Matt Cohen, and Alice Munro. It has been variously Eden, Purgatory, and Hell to these writers, and has acquired a quasi-mythical force. Although he has traveled in Europe—most recently in the spring of 1982—Hood has rooted most of his fiction in Ontario, whose place-names he celebrates for their rich mythological associations: "Guelph: the Holy Roman Empire and the Florentine struggle for liberty. Fergus, Arthur, Owen, all great Celtic heroes. . . . [Mt. Forest] is a land like the faerie kingdom of Spenser's poem, a forest mount, a dream glade where drawn-out enchantments elaborate themselves. The place—the little town and the country roundabout *are* precisely Spenserian in their mysterious slow beauty and calm" (*GB,* 66).

This facility for associations is part of what Hood calls "sportive play of the imagination,"[3] and it is deepened by his analytical and synthesizing powers of mind. Ever since childhood, it seems, Hood has had a fascination with bringing quantities of diverse material together and adjusting them in relationships. But the gift of curiosity and the process of inquiry require discipline, and Hood's Catholic background certainly helped in the formation of an active emblematic imagination.

In "Before the Flood,"[4] an autobiographical essay on the formative literary and nonliterary influences on his life, Hood shows that religion was the greatest grounding. The first element of a book that made a solid impression on him was not even print: it was a steel engraving of Jonah and the Whale, found in the Benziger Brothers'

Bible History, "issued in Baltimore before the beginning of the century by the noted Catholic publishers, and furnished in quantities to
ecclesiastical booksellers over the next fifty years."[5] His emblematic
imagination was stirred by the engraving, and as he absorbed biblical
legends and myths, the Scriptures stayed ineradicably in his mind.
Although he did not read the Old Testament seriously till he was
forty, he got "the necessary and absolute grounding" in it out of the
Benziger book. The New Testament entered by ear, not by eye. It
was read in sections at church, fifty-two Sundays a year, plus daily at
Lent, First Fridays, Holy Days of Obligation, and every day during
the weeks when he was appointed server at early Mass in the parish
church: "Reading through the Gospels, the Acts of the Apostles, the
Epistles, the Apocalypse, nowadays, I see that almost the whole of
the sacred text was read to us in the course of a few years, and how
it stuck!"[6]

   Equally sacral in meaning and tendency to him was Butler's *Catechism,* an abridgment of the renowned Baltimore *Catechism* "which
served as a manual of doctrine and devotion for a century of churchly
living in North America." It also served as "an elementary manual of
dialectic. Its question-and-answer format was appropriately ordered to
religious controversy." With its "precise formularies" in mind, he
felt he could confute in argument any of the Protestants on his block.
Yet, no part of this exclusive diet of Christian narrative and apolo-
getic seemed to him then in the least other-worldly, excessively pious
or grim, or remote from daily life. Nor did it in any way incite fears
of hellfire or pangs of terrified conscience. On the contrary, it encouraged "a lively, fascinated interest in wonderful stories and acute
but simply expressed perceptions of divinity."[7] Nothing else he read
at the same time or later made the same impact, and his other boyhood reading served to propose "subtle secular analogies of what was
to be found in Scripture or Catechism."[8]

   Hood was also influenced by children's literature from England
that illustrated codes of manliness, truthfulness, and cleanliness. The
pull of Empire was strong in these stories, which had "nothing Latin,
nothing southern, and no girls."[9] Young Hood was fascinated by
their "irrational and opaque code of manners, that of a group infi-
nitely foreign and exalted, much like the gods in Homer, incomprehensible, often silly and unjustifiable, but classy. . . ."[10]

   Away from books, Hood was "obscurely conscious of some sort of
moral void, some absence of code, or manners, to cover life from

Monday to Saturday. Sundays had the blessings of the Gospel, but the secular weekdays had to be filled with illustrated giftbooks that could address the boy's voracious curiosity and satisfy his insatiable appetite for fact. Cars, planes, and ships motored around his imagination, straight out of *The Wonder Book of Motors, The Wonder Book of the Navy,* and *The Book of Splendid Planes.* And it was from such books with their color plates that Hood derived most of his interest in emblems. Motorcar radiator badges, for instance, were precisely heraldic: "They derived from the formal and largely conventional figures of mediaeval heraldic design; their colours were those of chivalric blazonry, bright, unambiguous, specific, nothing to do with good taste, hierarchical, permanent, even liturgical."[11]

Hood found in these enameled and ornamented designs "a kind of exactitude, a poised, rather stiff formality which insistently recalled the Mass and the priestly vestments. Value, mystery, permanence; these were the elements of life evoked by the exactly defined forms of the radiator badges; there was something Byzantine about them, a timeless quietude beyond life which was unlike, say, totem, or anything animal. They were neither images nor symbols. They were emblems."[12] Getting into his teens, Hood could find a complex system of ritual distinctions—hieratic, liturgical, defined, coded, ranked precision of color, line, shape, value—everywhere in life and literature.

In the fall of 1947 he went to the University of Toronto, and a flood of learning and experience began. Writing a doctoral thesis in 1955, entitled "Theories of Imagination in English Thinkers 1650–1790," trained him to stay with a long work and taught him how not to overtire himself or go stale. His thesis was concerned with "the psychology of the imagination, particularly in the seventeenth and eighteenth century, and the views of the imagination which evolved in that period." It was a propadeutic to Romantic poetics, especially those of Wordsworth and Coleridge, and wound up arguing that "imagination and abstraction as Aristotle and St. Thomas understood them were really the same power of the soul, that scholastic and Thomistic notions of abstraction were penetrative and life-enhancing, vitalistic and not concerned to 'murder to dissect' but on the other hand to comprehend fully and to rejoice in the nature of the things they contemplated."[13] This thesis established Hood's opposition to Cartesian dualism, where conceptual reality becomes the only reality, or where there is a radical cleavage between mind and body. Hood is a monist who, like Aquinas in philosophy, would describe the intellectual soul as the form of the body, which depends on the body for sense knowledge. The thesis was an academic expression of his preoccupations with himself as an artist.

Graduate study at Toronto also pointed him in the direction of allegory. A course in Spenser given by the renowned A. S. P. Woodhouse became a landmark in his intellectual and aesthetic development. It showed Hood that there was a through-line from Boethius, Dante, Spenser, and the Bible to the literature that he was beginning to write. True to his monistic vision, however, Hood found himself more committed to Dantean allegory than to Spenserian, for the Dantean type was "very much more able to save this world, and to preserve this world, than Spenserian." Spenser was deemed to be "dualistic and Platonist and to have not as substantial an awareness of the fleshly solidity of things."[14]

After his doctorate, Hood had to cross the United States border to find a job: "A. S. P. Woodhouse controlled English education in Canada, and if you got a job you got it through him. He was very kind to me but he could see that there was something funny about me—that I was really an artist and not a scholar."[15] Hood taught at at a small women's Catholic college, St. Joseph's, in Connecticut, until 1961, when he was offered a post at the University of Montreal. He accepted gladly, partly because it presented an opportunity to be where half his roots were. However, he had to overcome the temptation to be assistant fiction editor at *Esquire* before the move.

In Montreal with his wife, the artist Noreen Mallory (who had been on the very first costume-designing crew at the Stratford Festival), and their four university-age children (Sarah, Dwight, John, and Alexandra), Hood lives on a quiet, shaded street in Notre Dame de Grace. He has passed his thirtieth year of teaching, and has already supervised more than a hundred masters' and doctoral theses. Fluently bilingual, he is one of the few Canadian writers who does not ignore the French fact in Quebec, and although he is not in full sympathy with the political and cultural aspirations of French Quebec, his work does attempt to reconcile his conscience with that of French Canada. As early as 1964, following the publication of his first novel, he announced his aim to unite the whole of Canadian bilingual culture, however imperfect the style of his written French.[16]

Hood's writing career only took off after the death of his father in 1959: "Some kind of dammed-up body material was released. I got very hot and wrote about fourteen stories in fourteen months and sold every one of them." Most of the early stories are collected in his first book, *Flying a Red Kite,* which was published in an edition of 1,100 copies and went out of print in eighteen months. This book brought him a $200 award from the Toronto Women's Canada Club in 1963, and his short fiction continued to appear in numerous journals. Citations came in *The Yearbook of the American Short Story* and *Distinctive Short Stories in America Magazine* in 1961 and 1967. Moreover, Hood won the President's Medal from the University of Western Ontario in 1963 for "The End of It."[17]

Yet, Hood does not like to be designated primarily as a writer of short stories. Two early attempts at a novel, *God Rest You Merry* and *Hungry Generations,* did not succeed and remain unpublished, but Hood kept working at his craft, moving from fiction to journalism and back again. He had been fashioning semidocumentary pieces for his urban pastoral, *Around the Mountain: Scenes from Montreal Life,* when Robert Weaver and John Robert Colombo asked him to be their man at Expo '67 for the *Tamarack Review.* In "Circuses And Bread" (*GB,* 21–34), he showed it was possible to reconcile conscience and pleasure at the same time—something that went against the spirit of Canadian puritanism. His first mass-circulation assignment came in September of that year, when Peter Gzowski, editor then of *Star Weekly,* asked him to do a story about expansion teams in the National Hockey League. Hood, a player in the amateur Sportsmen's Hockey League (along with his close friend the artist Seymour Segal), was in his element—just as he would be twelve years later when he did the text to accompany Segal's eighteen hockey paintings that expressed sex and violence in the sport.

His journalism and fiction have always converged. His experience in team sport found expression in *A Game of Touch,* and the excitement of bridges and ravines charges parts of *The Swing in the Garden.* Much of *Around the Mountain* also seems to be autobiographical, although the book is meant to be fiction. Hood believes that a good journalist is one who has learned his lessons well from fiction: "A good writer of fiction is disciplined to observe carefully and to arrange patterns of social behaviour in artistic form with a degree of finesse beyond that of any journalist I can think of. It's because Mailer and Baldwin have written fiction that they, and Turgenev and Hemingway too, have become good journalists" (*GB,* 108).

Hood's literary career is often treated as if it were composed of two

uneven halves—the fictive and the journalistic. Some critics have
been quick to accept Robert Fulford's canard, fabricated after the
publication of *The Camera Always Lies* in 1967, that almost everything Hood writes in nonfiction has a "sharp, clear, truthful ring,"
whereas almost everything he writes in long fiction is "dull, flat and
spiritless," when it isn't simply "embarrassingly pretentious."[18]

On balance, however, Hood has more supporters than detractors.
He has been called "one of the most accomplished of his generation
in the art of invisible craftsmanship."[19] His surface, we are told,
masks "much deeper truths" than are apparent at first.[20] It has been
argued that the primary intent of his novels is "to comprehend the
ultimate nature of reality, the ontology of being, on a scale that includes the spiritual without demeaning the mundane and ordinary."[21]
Hood has been called Proustian,[22] Balzacian,[23] as well as "Canada's
most learned, most intellectual writer"[24]—a "mind-stretcher" who
"attempts dimensions in his fiction which most writers would just as
soon experience for themselves in somebody else's work."[25]

When he first began writing fiction, Hood had no literary theory
and belonged to no school. Instinctively he turned out to be "a moral
realist, not a naturalist nor a surrealist or advance guard writer" (*GB*,
127). All his early writing deals with "credible characters in more or
less credible situations," and what they show us are human relationships in continually shifting phases. But the greatest thing they show
is where the human joins with the divine, and, thereby, they are diverse panels about human existence, rounded off as a comedy of salvation. However, this salvation is not always attained. Paths to it are
fraught with temptations that delay, interrupt, or sometimes even
end the pilgrimage.

Hood's Catholicism infuses hope into his art, and, with his monism, allows him to see life and art as a continuous relationship shot
through with trinitarian structures. The three highest forms of human activity for him are religious worship, art, and love,[26] and all his
fiction makes a single tapestry of these three interrelated motifs.

Because his emphasis is on hope, grace, and redemption, his critics
say his art lacks drama and an adequate sense of evil. But Hood does
not like the "artificiality" of dramatic forms, and he does not see suffering as a means to redemption: "Life isn't dramatic. It's saved. The
battle is over. You have to win salvation in your own life, but the
world isn't going to fall apart. The world is held up by a very powerful creative force. That's not a dramatic action; that's a glorious
action."[27]

His epical New Age series, designed to be a work that reflects the intellectual, social, literary, political, and economic history of Canada's twentieth century from the end of World War I to the year 1999, when the final volume is to be published, will have the design of a divinely human comedy. It already shows influences by Dante, Coleridge, Joyce, Proust, and Anthony Powell,[28] but it is meant to be multi-modal, encyclopedic, and a true Canadian epic that puts his own country visibly at the center of a massive fiction. Taking a cue from Harold A. Innis, the author of major pioneer works on communication, transport, and technology, Hood makes railways, banks, and mail-order catalogs three of his dominant epic motifs, and with his memory serving as a mother to his muse of fiction, he tries to create the conscience of Canada. Story, which Hood regards as being very close to liturgy and "the permanent possession of mankind" (*GB,* 112), is here turned into long associative chains bound firmly around the theme of moral redemption.

How does an author decide to compose a twelve-part epic? Hood once explained: "Well, it's got to do with immortality. Remember that line in Hazlitt? No man in youth believes that he will ever die. I think the fact of mortality has got to me."[29] He has never been modest in his ambitions, and yearns to be a Canadian artist who "could move easily and in a familiar converse with Joyce, and Tolstoy, and Proust."[30] He wants to give the rest of his life to being that kind of artist.

Chapter Two
The Short Stories

Emblematic Imagination and Allegorical Mode

As a Catholic, Hood cannot help making the redemption of man a central creed in his fiction. The theme is not turned into a sectarian inquiry, however. Redemption becomes something available to everyone, no matter what his natural talents or opportunities, his psychic or cultural development. Catholic theology is a moral force that implicitly informs his deepest vision. The moral tone is high, but without being injunctive or doctrinaire. Hood espouses without preachment; he observes without necessarily forcing issues or moral victories. Yet, by some special balance in his craft, he is always interpretive—never simply a passive documentarian. And sharpening this sense of significance is a strong physical form for the fiction. Sometimes this sense of form becomes a game with numerologies. Most often, however, it is intrinsic and is crystallized by the device of the emblem.

An emblem is distinct from a symbol. Both are iconic embodiments of thought and feeling, but while a symbol "at once reveals and conceals,"[1] an emblem is a visual design that is a speaking picture—more precise than a symbol but no less effective in its ability to mediate between the physical and the divine. An emblem and a symbol are both analogies for reality, but a symbol is a metaphor "one half of which remains unstated and indefinite,"[2] whereas an emblem, deriving as it does from hieroglyphics, is always particular, though it can vary in character from the explicit allegory of an Aesopian fable to the enigmatic subtlety of a metaphysical conceit in John Donne's poetry. Where a symbol, because it is a figure or an image used as the sign of something, is primarily aesthetic,[3] an emblem combines the beautiful with the didactically moral. Both symbol and emblem share, however, the power to externalize the hidden. Religious symbolism and Christian emblems both flourish as handmaidens of the supernatural, and in Hood everything expresses the divine signature.

As with Baudelaire (who in "Correspondances" makes the poet a seer who sees into the infinite), Hood practices a method of reaching a vision in which the reader can participate. Also, like Emanuel Swedenborg, Hood believes in a reciprocity between the natural and spiritual worlds. But for Hood the code of this emblematic correspondence is not hermetic; it is a profound but apprehensible language whereby the infinite addresses the finite.

Hood's emblems are numerous: a Halloween gorilla-mask; a mountain overlooking a metropolis; a sunken "ghost" ship; an oil painting of white light; garden swing; an Olympic stadium whose "O" shape is an analogy for nothingness. The list could go on intriguingly, but it is sufficient to say that this iconography of the imagination produces an allegorical mode which is an extension of literary symbolism.

When Hood first came to critical attention in 1962, he was praised condescendingly for his "sound English" and marvelous sense of place, as if the only criteria for literary distinction were correct grammar and a regional ambience. Not many critics read him according to the conventions he was using, and so did not know how to deal with him. While Ronald Sutherland and Robert Fulford rushed to proclaim him as part of the Canadian mainstream, Margaret Atwood and Doug Jones ignored him altogether in their descriptive grids for Canadian literature. He was lumped by A. J. M. Smith together with Sinclair Ross, Hugh Garner, Jack Ludwig, Mordecai Richler, and Alice Munro for realism and a "peculiar amalgam of irony and sentiment,"[4] which was really quite a startling lump considering the many radical ways in which Hood differs from these writers. There are still too many critics and reviewers who refuse to believe that he writes something other than sheer realism. Even in 1980 it was possible to find a reviewer who could write with touching innocence of Hood's natural "figures of speech" drawn from "physical geography."[5]

Hood has spoken so frequently about his allegorical method that a critic who does not read his fiction as allegory is either inordinately perverse or helplessly naive. Northrop Frye contends that "genuine allegory is a structural element in literature"[6] and that commentary itself is "allegorical interpretation, an attaching of ideas to the structure of poetic imagery."[7] So it is certainly not inappropriate to undertake an allegorical interpretation of Hood, a writer who, in trying to "assimilate the mode of the novel to the mode of fully-developed Christian allegory," believes that he is "more 'real' than the realists, yet more transcendent than the most vaporous allegorist."[8] Hood follows what he conceives as the synchronous method of Dante.[9] His fiction creates relationships with the gospels and biblical parables, and he is one of few novelists who are concerned with the holy life or the life of grace. Those who would object to a reading of Hood's fiction as religious allegory have less of a quarrel with literary criticism than with the genesis of literature itself. They forget that "the origins of allegory are philosophic and theological rather than literary. Most of all perhaps they are religious."[10]

The world of classical antiquity provides us with abundant evidence of religion finding its perfect expression in narrative that combines a psychic level with the material, as in the myths of Demeter and Persephone, Leda and the swan, the rape of Europa, or Orpheus and Eurydice. Even Virgil's *Aeneid,* not ostensibly a religious narrative, is "an allegory of the dark night of the soul as it is tempered to become the instrument of divine purpose."[11]

It was Christianity, however, that truly widened the use of allegory and made it the general foundation of narrative. Figural and narrative allegory, so common in ancient Greece and Rome, became common types in the Bible, although the most characteristic form became typological allegory, "a New Testament exegetic method which treated events and figures of the Old Testament as combining historical reality with prophetic meanings in terms of the Gospels and the Christian dispensation."[12] Old Testament events and personages became "types" or figurae of New Testament events and personages, so that it was characteristic of this method to read Christ as the second Adam, or the manna in the desert as a correspondence to the Eucharist, or Moses as a prefigurement of Christ, or the Song of Solomon as an allegory of the mutual love of Christ and the Church. The new point of view saw history as a process, directed by God from Creation and the Fall toward the Incarnation, Redemption, and, finally, the Apocalypse.

Hood's allegory in its full emblematic force is not a primitive species of cyphering. It is not at all like medieval allegory or naive allegory where ideas are always their images, and where criticism has to apply itself to the text as if to a document. It never loses its sensory appeal or allows its inner meaning to antagonize the literal reality under and through which the signification is maintained. Hood's allegory is a convention by which *inner* drama of conscience or soul is revealed in a discursive narrative, and it fluently reconciles emblem with idea. Fiction and idea are always in continuous emblematic interdependence. In this way, Hood's fiction is expansive rather than narrow, and its deliberate didacticism in no way seeks to reveal by minute dissection. The narrative is always coherent, never suffocated by what Erich Auerbach calls "the vines of allegory."[13]

Hood has an allegorical imagination that is able to bring together various meanings at a single moment of action, by conducting correspondences of the natural to the supernatural, for instance, or of the low to the high, of time to eternity. His purpose is to show what humans are capable of, with as many associations or patterns as his own mind can make. He starts with the commonest of things, and his images are natural, perhaps even inevitable—streets, buildings, and geography he has known, people he has observed, the two languages he has been formed by. In these things the significant emblems emerge; from them the divinely human comedy takes shape; by them he rounds off a meaning for his fiction. Nature yields to his powerful analytical and synthesizing mind, but Hood, for all his pursuit of the Divine Essence in common and uncommon history, does not shatter man's commitment to the physical world.

Hood's allegory demonstrates a familiar paradox where "the generalities of allegory acquire power over the moral sense and the imagination by way of their relevance to the particular."[14] While his analogies and emblems sometimes yield static meditations, they are rooted in actions that are never pulverized into ghostly departed quantities. His imagination never becomes what Allen Tate has called "the angelic mind"—a mentality that, in its quest after direct knowledge of essences, denies man's commitment to the physical world, and sets itself up in "quasi-divine independence."[15] What Tate perceives in Dante's symbolic imagination is what we can comment on concerning Hood's emblematic imagination. His fullest image is "an action in the shapes of this world: it does not reject, it includes; it sees not only with but through the natural world, to what may lie beyond it. Its humility is witnessed by its modesty. It never begins at the top; it carries the bottom along with it, however high it may climb."[16]

Flying a Red Kite

From his very first book of short stories, Hood's emblems have shaped ideas and structures. The title story in *Flying a Red Kite*[17] turns the human spirit into a sacramental which is no sham. It begins with signs of things gone awry—sometimes in comically grotesque

images. The main character, Fred Calvert (whose surname forms an
association with Calvary), is riding home on a bus one hot Saturday
afternoon. The ride begins badly as Fred, encumbered by parcels,
queues up for the wrong bus, which waddles up "like an indecent old
cow" that stops "with an expiring moo" (FRK, 176). Fred has to join
another queue and wait under the "right sign." Fred and his wife,
Naomi (another biblical association), had "thought of Montreal as a
city of the Sub-Arctic and in the summers they would have leisure to
repent the misjudgment" (FRK, 177). We learn of Fred's boyhood
failures in fishing and hockey, and of how, as "one by one the whole-
some outdoor sports and games had defeated him," he had transferred
his belief in sports to his young daughter, Deedee.

The mood of frustration continues as he climbs into a crowded bus.
An Irish priest (one of two loud, vulgar revelers) mutters, "It's all a
sham" as the bus passes a cemetery (FRK, 181). Fred's depression is
not cured at home. A drink of Coke bloats him and upsets his stom-
ach; he regrets having bought a red kite for his daughter; the "spoiled
priest" stays in his mind; and it is the wrong weather for kite-flying.

All the portents of wrongdoing or infelicity are linked to a sequence of passions for Fred. He and his daughter start up a mountain, and Fred makes a covenant with her, not to come down until
they have flown the kite. The ascent makes him victim to a scourge
of bugs, and he twice fails to launch the kite, his "natural symbol"
of something holy (FRK, 178). He ascends higher than he has ever
been before, and the weather, now changed into dazzling sunshine,
dry and clear, is perfect for his pastoral pastime. Deedee finds a wild
raspberry bush and eats from it, relishing the fruit, which is not bitter. As trickles of dark juice run down her chin, Fred, on his third
attempt, manages to loft the kite, which soars up and up. The flying
kite and "the dark rich red of the pulp and juice of the crushed rasp-
berries" become complementary natural symbols of grace or benediction as Fred realizes in a flash that the "spoiled priest," who claimed
that life and monuments to immortality were a sham, was wrong.
The resurrection of the red kite (a tongue of fire, as it were, whose
string burns his fingers) matches the resurrection of Fred's spirit
(FRK, 188).

The act of flying the kite becomes an analogy of faith for Fred because his various empirical crises pass away at the moment of the
kite's soaring, and this becomes the climactic epiphany in the story—
a gift of the spirit that meets its challenges without yielding. The

kite now is, indeed, something holy, for it joins heaven to earth via the ball of string and brings a feeling of accomplishment and peace to Fred (whose name, by the way, is etymologically related to "peace"). The kite-flying justifies Fred's belief in the "curative moral values" of sports and games, and heals his discomfort over the "spoiled priest's" cynicism. As he and his daughter kneel and embrace in the dust and squint at "the flying red thing," his spiritual passion is relieved and he is regenerated, as it were, through signs of grace: faith, the Spirit (the kite's ribs form a cross), and sacramental water/blood (the berry juice).

Most of the other stories in the book coalesce around two complementary themes—various gifts of the spirit, and the alarming "doubleness" in life. The "doubleness" can produce a disturbing ambiguity, as in "Nobody's Going Anywhere!" (*FRK*, 158–75), with a teasing image of black comedy as an emblematic "talisman," or it can give rise to a comedy of manners as in "He Just Adores Her!" (*FRK*, pp. 136–57), where the "doubleness" arises out of the bipartite structure and tension between the love of one couple and the envy of another.

Hood's success in the short story obtains to a large extent from his attention to texture. The literal documentary approach in "Recollections of the Works Department" (*FRK*, 63–98) chronicles a season of manual labor. This story, set in the spring and summer of 1952, refuses to be dated. Much anthologized, it has a freshness in its good humor, easy observation, and benign satire. It begins casually (the way Hood often begins his fiction) but the innocent, peaceful languor is not permanent. The narrator, a graduate student, becomes a laborer in the Toronto Roadways Division and has to deal with blue-collar hostility to his university education. He knows nothing about the rigors of shoveling or the conflicts among the work crew, but he learns quickly and soon adapts to the "cityese" folk around him. There is nothing pretentious about his recounting, and the occasional flirtations with the jocund are diversionary without being superfluous. They carry us into a world that invites special participation, but they do not strain to become an elaborate myth of the working class. The narrator knows his own limits as a documentarian and individual, and he observes these limits wisely. We see in his historical impulse the sort of power that later informs the New Age series.

Another short-story memoir crystallizes its own moral around an heraldic emblem. "Silver Bugles, Cymbals, Golden Silks" (*FRK*, 40–

62) shows how the gift of mature love preserves the myth of the past once time has faded old reality. Here Hood is definitely out to create a pastoralism in decline, with remembered summer-camp lore and all the rituals of flag-raising and bugle-retreat. But the point is analogical. His ideal as a youth is to be a part of the Oakdale Boys Band, whose splendid uniforms of gold and glittering silk fill him with awe. The story becomes a recitation of the Band's history—a history of decline and corruption. The gold uniforms fade, the music deteriorates, the manners of the musicians fall into disrepute. And yet in the "changing light" of time, the "past glories, things that are utterly vanished, that will never come back again," do acquire a real value that is not merely sentimental. The narrator's tender love for the past leaders of the band is genuine and healing.

Nowhere in this book is Hood's sense of texture and structure so brilliantly in evidence, however, as in "Fallings From Us, Vanishings" (*FRK*, 1–17). On the surface, this is a story of how a young man loves not only a girl but her mother and a whole host of memories as well. But it is much more than a Wordsworthian lyrical exercise. Wordsworth inspires the title and some of the emblematic suggestions, but the piece is really a Grail story where the Arthur figure is quite literally an Arthur who goes in quest of all the glory in things, past, present, and future.

The title comes from the "Intimations of Immortality Ode" and suggests decline and evanescence—a ghostliness that somehow does not vitiate the material substantiality of experience. But more than Wordsworth, the story suggests medieval legend and emblem. It begins with the protagonist, Arthur Merlin (whose names connote questing king and magician), "brandishing a cornucopia of daffodils, flowers for Gloria" (*FRK*, 1). The cornucopia ("horn of plenty") is here a golden cup because it holds the bright yellow daffodils— Wordsworth's symbol of lyric exultation. In legend, a cornucopia is Jupiter's cup, and Hood fills his opening paragraph with emblems of Jupiter in the fertility and arboreal images. Hood also maintains the element of romance so that the mood helps to color the deeper thematic underpinnings.

Gloria lets us remember Wordsworth's "clouds of glory" and "glory in the flower," especially when Merlin hands her the daffodils and watches her bury her face in the petals. She is "the daffodil girl, the primavera" (*FRK*, 7). She wears a "flowery robe" and daffodils are "her favorite flower" (*FRK*, 8), so she is Merlin's golden one. But there is an illusion here—just as there were ghostly, wandering fires in the Grail legend. She is unattainable because she is a "ghost" who haunts Arthur, no less than she is haunted by the "ghosts" of the past. Indeed, her "ghostliness" forms an important part of the central leitmotif where time quivers without being forgotten or laid to rest in the mind or soul.

Gloria would prefer to forget the past because it holds too many tragic memories for her. Her father had died in a sinking ship, and she cannot accept Arthur's sacral association for water (*FRK*, 10). Nor does she wish to remember her mother's death in a car smashup. Gloria would much rather live in the present and place her trust in the senses, which help her experience concrete particulars rather than abstract generalizations. "I only see what's there," she maintains once to Arthur (*FRK*, 11), and her state of being is frequently described in terms of the external senses of touch, taste, and sight.

In contrast, Arthur is tense with memory, but grateful for it. An historian, "builder of archives, ranker of green filing cabinets," he loves documents and relishes the past (*FRK*, 5). He does not censor experience or memory, and his sense of period provides the documentary relish in the story. He has the gift of triple vision in the sense of his mental presence in three levels of time.

On the allegorical level, the story is a version of time and feeling, and of Arthur's magical (Merlinesque) reconciliation of the two. As a boy, he had adored Gloria's mother, Mrs. Vere, "that golden widow" (*FRK*, 4), whose name etymologically means "the truth." But she's a part of his past, and his present involvement is with Gloria, his glory in the present, who cannot or will not connect the triple levels of time. She is thereby haunted, "packed full of sensation" almost exclusively from time present, and he cannot exorcize her of her spiritual demons, although she appeals to the magician in him: "You exorcist! Just come and get me!" (*FRK*, 16). What to her is an unsettling possession is to him a beneficent condition. Their dialogue here does sound melodramatic and arch at times, but it is Hood's way of signaling his didactic intent and of building to an emotional climax.

The final paragraph is quieter, lyrical, and poignant as Gloria disappears, merging with the twilight, wavering away—one of "a long file of daffodil girls marching out of the past and into the future." As the title shows, she vanishes, and by being one of "the descending heirs of Eve" she falls away from him (*FRK*, 17). His eyes lose her, just as King Arthur's eyes lost the Holy Grail, but Arthur Merlin does not lose his feeling for or idea of her. Although his setting acquires the image of a wasteland ("a sandy place"), he is content and blessed with his memories.

The pattern of light and darkness merges with the theme of decline. Arthur's yearning to see Gloria "illuminated by the sunset" occurs on "nearly the longest day of the year" (FRK, 5). All through their beach encounter that fades into the "dying sunlight" (FRK, 7) Arthur is very conscious of disappearing light and the oncoming twilight. The sun throws a shadow across them, and the sand under them grows black and loses its daytime warmth (FRK, 12). "The soul of the world turns in on itself and is quiet, just before the dark" (FRK, 13): Arthur is ever conscious of the passage of time. Gloria's final merging with the twilight occurs after a phase of sexual yearning, and seals the pattern of ghost-ridden beauty "going out of the light through the twilight and into the dark" (FRK, 17). Her going, however, is a thing of beauty that quivers with a twinge of glory and is, therefore, reminiscent of Wordsworth's "cloud of glory."

Another story equally impressive in its synecdoche is "Three Halves of a House" (FRK, 99–123), and this, too, is a version of ghostliness as it tells its own tale of possession. It begins as a geographical documentary as Hood, with conversational ease, conducts us on a guided tour of Thousand Islands. The islands "sprout in and all around the ship channel, choking and diverting the immense river for forty amazing miles . . . a third of the continent leans pushing behind the lakes and the river" (FRK, 99). The images of a human body ("pulse, circulation, artery, and heart") all fortify the sense of palpable, living force.

Hood shifts his narrative voice frequently in the story, modulating the tone and strengthening the sense of aesthetic distance. Soon after his description of the islands comes a description of the oceangoing freighters, and then he brings in the theme of ruin and decline via third-person, objective narrative. This is virtually a Gothic story, quasi-Faulknerian in its sense of the land and its haunting spirit. It is a tale of ancestral conflicts and madness. The house of the title is occupied by Grover Haskell and his insane wife, Ellie, but Mrs. Boston insists that it belongs to her and her daughter, Maura.

The story works up to the special knowledge obtained by Maura and the mad Ellie, and Hood uses the image of eyes in order to emphasize the haunting spirit of ruin and dispossession. Ellie has violet eyes that give her an "ineffable saint's gaze, visionary, violet, preoccupied." She yearns for Maura to be her daughter figure, and though she seems quite crazy in her behavior, she is considered a religious visionary who speaks in symbols and who has "second sight" (*FRK*, 110). Only Maura can see the true pathos in the situation, for her mother's "agate eyes" are cold and unclear.

The ghost of Ellie's "terrible father" still hovers about the house, which has a spectral, icy form in winter. Ellie sees the ghost of an unborn daughter in Maura, and Mrs. Boston sees the ghost of her husband in the house, as the house itself becomes unearthly, taking possession of the neurotic relatives—even those who wish to be dispossessed of it.

Ellie, who believes the house is haunted by ghosts, turns into something of a ghost herself, moving with "no footfall," passing soundlessly in Maura's memory (*FRK*, 115). When Ellie embraces Maura, the latter can hardly feel her hug and thinks of her aunt as "an invisible tissue of air."

The most haunted figures are Ellie and her husband, Grover Haskell. Contrary to Mrs. Boston's conception of him, Grover does not want the house, which is killing him as surely as the river is strangling Stoverville. He actually pleads with Maura to accept the place from him (*FRK*, 122). For her part, Ellie is haunted by several things which have become the ghosts of her tormented conscience. Her unrequited passion for Wallace Phillips has made her covetous of the Phillips daughter. She glares at Maura and says: "You'd have been my child and you *are* my child though you won't admit it" (*FRK*, 117). Her life in the house becomes a harrowing punishment decreed by the gods and the dead. She continues to see her dead father and to hear his command forbidding her to marry Grover.

Hood's narrative voice switches again in the final section to get inside Ellie's "milky brains." In her bedroom, which is a bizarre synthesis of virgin womb, nun's cloister, and tomb, she goes through the mimesis of a woman in childbirth. But what is born is not even a phantom child—it is an eternal now, carrying the story full circle with its images of water, ships, and sirens. The strong landscape, a frame for the story, is internalized within Ellie's disintegrating mind, and the conclusion reveals a special ghostliness—a voyage unto death, as the dying Ellie's dissolving mind flows like the river current of Anna Livia Plurabelle in Joyce's *Finnegans Wake*.

The ending is apocalyptic in its symbolism. Many of the elements (seven stars, seven coronets, the trees, and river as mouth) are drawn from the Book of Revelation, for Hood's point here appears to be a special vision for Ellie as her soul travels to its final translation. Her inner voice is identified with that of the river, and she is swallowed up by eternity as she goes to meet her Redeemer.

Secular redemption is offered to Maura, who is the only one to survive in life the ghostly haunting and ruin. Because she succeeds in making a career for herself in Montreal, she prevents a family pattern of destruction from repeating itself in her life. When she returns to Stoverville, it is only a temporary visit. She feels no fatal ties. She is not like Grover, who is "an outsider who's gotten stuck fast inside" (FRK, 113).

Flying a Red Kite is such a virtuoso performance that it is hard to believe it is a beginner's collection. The emblems are organizing principles rather than sheer symbolic elements, and the apocalyptic endings obtain a special force. Unlike those writers whose cynicism turns into a peculiar sentimentality of revolt, Hood offers a hard-centered optimism that holds because of his technical sincerity. This allegorist suffers from no anemia of the imagination. While it is true that at his worst he touches melodrama, he possesses a poetic sensibility and a vision that is refreshingly different from that of anyone else. He sharpens our hunger for truth in the fascinating guise of fiction, before feeding us with apocalypse.

Hood is the type of literary craftsman who believes in shaping all his work into a single piece. For him, stories and novels are "slices off the same ham,"[18] and although his literary reputation has been made chiefly on his short stories, he makes no distinction in importance between his long and short fiction, suggesting that all his books make up "one huge novel anyway, the one bright book of the redemption and atonement."[19] It is not that he repeats the same stories or that he is technically limited. It is simply that his themes and essential style have not changed radically, though there have been widenings, focal alterations, and varnishings of his emblematic form. As *Flying a Red Kite* shows, he has never had to learn to wipe his feet before entering the salon of superior fiction-makers, and each new collection of short stories simply consolidates his emblematic style. His idea is that "underlying everything there is some kind of intelligible and meaningful unity" which he rounds off in stories that tend to coalesce in groups or assimilate themselves into larger fictions.[20]

Around the Mountain

Around the Mountain: Scenes from Montreal Life[21] shows how Hood's documentary talent unites with literary skill to yield a mode of journalistic literature that is a rich mixture of scenes, sketches, incidents, and full-fledged stories. Hood's documentary eye is as apt to take in a political riot in a public park ("One Way North and South"—*AM,* 95–111) as it is beguilingly drawn to mysterious characters who become obsessions to others ("A Green Child"—*AM,* 127–39). A strong heart, unabashed sentimentality, and a wide mind capable of subtle associations become valuable gifts to the writer.

Although subtitled "Scenes from Montreal Life," this book is not mere photographic documentary realism. The twelve stories (each centered in a different calendar month) form a cycle that is more than calendar art. They are located in fascinating environments, and their various emblems signal a mythology of place. In them, everything connects: topography, sociology, history, religion, politics, sport, art. Hood's narrative facility develops from the exigencies of life around him:

"Where do you get your ideas from anyway?"
There's an answer to that question but it never satisfies anybody. However, I gave it to them in all its banality.
"All around me; there's a story in everybody around us." (*AM,* 148)

Hood's craft takes ordinary situations and by the slightest pressure or rearrangement brings patterns to the surface.

Around the Mountain fuses Hood's documentary talent with his emblematic mode in a perfect harmony of revelations. The very title and chapter divisions make it abundantly clear that this is not a mere sketch book in the manner of Turgenev's *A Sportsman's Sketches* or Dickens's *Sketches by Boz* or George Eliot's *Scenes of Clerical Life*. The title implies a focus for epiphany. Mountains, because of their elevation, are sites of refined insights, transcendental truths, pure revelations. They provide a vantage point of superior perception. Hood indicates that his revelations will cluster around this symbol.

The mountain is Mount Royal—the very source for the place-name, Montreal. Many of the stories trace patterns of ascent and descent; many, too, mention the qualities of vision, modes of knowing that are altered by geographical position or weather. ("Fair weather

implies heightened perception . . ." [*AM,* 81].) Though the early
stories are set in the city, at low sea-level, there are frequent references to climbing and descending, to snow and fog, rain and sun,
and as the weather, location, and color alter, so do the author's vision
and our insights. As Hood himself explains:

The stories begin on the flat land up in the northeast of the Montreal region
and they gradually make their way up to the top. In the June story they're
at the top looking down from above, and that is, if you like, the holiest
story. . . . Then it winds around the mountain and back down to the flat
land north of Montreal but this time in the west. A complete rotation
around the mountain from east to west takes place, and the stories are calculated to how high up the mountain they are.[22]

There are calculations even in the narrative voice. The narrator
changes. One story has no first-person pronouns and is a third-person,
distanced story. In some of the other stories, the narrator is called
Hugh. Some of the stories are autobiographical; others are not.

The twelve stories form a year's circle, though not every chapter is
set in a single month. Chapter 1, for instance, begins in mid-December, but Chapter 2 ends in February, without mention of January.
Each of the other stories manages to find a different calendar month
for itself, though in some instances months overlap, and at the end
we return to mid-December. This structure achieves several things:
it shapes the book somewhat along the lines of Spenser's *Shepheardes
Calendar* or the Duc de Berri's *Book of Hours.*[23] It makes the stories
part of a natural cycle and, hence, part of a natural ritual. It provides
a scaffolding for Hood's emblematic imagination. And it makes a
clever mythology out of the banal, without any inordinate literary or
moral pressure.

The opening piece, "The Sportive Center of Saint Vincent de Paul"
(*AM,* 1–20), uses ice-hockey lore as a coloring and anecdotal device
in order to touch on the ritualistic and ethical aspects of a simple
pleasure. There is a "high moral line" which is mocked, so that the
tone never becomes pontifical or self-righteous.

Hockey is a slippery game played on ice, and *Around the Mountain*
has its various icy settings that help to freeze moments of revelation
without deadening the narrative or congealing the central idea. The
eleventh and twelfth stories carry us back to the winter season, moving from a bleak vision of political intrigue and cruelty in "Predic-
tions of Ice" (*AM,* 155–66) to a climactic revelation in the final

story, "The River Behind Things" (*AM*, 167–75). The "solitary black figure" with a long black pole jabbing the ice becomes an emblem of death, as vapor wraps around him. Hood tells us that he experienced such a figure himself, and that he was immediately reminded of the little black Dance of Death figure in paintings of Brueghel or Hieronymus Bosch.[24] Capitalizing on this association, he creates a poetic complex of hills, mystical experience, fog, snow, dark figure, death. In his eyes, the moment becomes virtually purgatorial in an eerie way:

Everything in my range of vision was softened or obscured by mist, except those agitated thin black limbs. I raised my eyes to the source of the river, several miles westwards where the lake contracts. Shore, water, air were all enveloped and changed, the city inexistent. Far off northwest, the high hills rose ghostly from the melting ice and snow. (*AM*, 175)

This is the type of meditative emblem so mastered by Wordsworth—who expressed it in the leech gatherer, the daffodils, the solitary reaper—but in Hood's transforming art, it wipes away the city teeming with its thousands of stories and leaves us with solitary man making a single-minded effort to clear a place for himself near the river, under the mountain.

There is a small element of the grotesque in Hood—such as the hideously deformed old woman in "Looking Down From Above" (*AM*, 81–94)—but his humanism enables him to soften the grotesque. "Looking Down From Above" is a model of his symmetry and depth. The ugly, dwarfish old lady struggling up a steep city street appears to have none of the advantages given to another key character in the story, M. Bourbonnais, a janitor who works hard for his pleasures, which he enjoys thoroughly. But fate strikes Bourbonnais with cancer, and his modest family picnic in June on the mountain becomes a sort of last supper in which the narrator accidentally, but fortuitously, shares. There is a tender scene of pastoral celebration, tinged with a foretaste of tragedy. The narrator, who obviously admires the dying man for his greatly energetic persistence in working for and enjoying worldly pleasures, leaves the family and climbs to the summit, from where he can survey the whole city below. The view provides "the sense of the world dropping away" (*AM*, 93)—a symbolic correspondence to the narrator's feeling at the brink of eternity (*AM*, 94). The world-view encompasses all the human perspectives, including Bourbonnais's contentment and the old lady's doggedness. Every human has his right to life in whatever measure of perception he can use. This moral synthesis projects the lesson that "human purpose is inscrutable, but undeniable" (*AM*, 94).

The pastoral moment in this story brings up the issue of the book's dominant mode. Hood himself calls *Around the Mountain* his "urban pastoral" because it presents correspondences to countryside, flowery meads, and pastoral activities.[25] He attempts to write a pastoral about Montreal which mediates between Stephen Leacock's nostalgia and Bertolt Brecht's infernal inversions. His city contains elements of both corruption and innocence, but is never purely hellish or paradisal. "A Green Child," where the narrator talks about the symbolic landscape of Antonioni's films of alienation, gives us the edge of the city, whose huge, unfinished building constructions look colossally impersonal and apocalyptic. The narrator descends into a valley of shadows (rue Valdombre) in quest of his fleeting green child, a girl with a green scarf, and here the green color and vanishing illumination are emblems of the grail light. But at the opposite end of this finally frustrating story is quite clearly the refreshingly innocent peace in the last story, where Hood and his young son, Dwight, drive out to the west island and find simple pleasures. Such contrasts attest to Hood's balancing act, which shows us multiple ways of looking at the same subject. And what is particularly subtle about this mode of vision is that it is not ironic or dualistic, but revelatory and monistic. It is all one city, and though we see Wordsworthian "spots of time" in calm scenes that "rest in one's faculties," stay, rotate, restate themselves repeatedly in "changing colours and meanings, exciting feelings, instincts, memory, imagination, seeming to have special powers to enlighten and give form to the rest of our lives" (*AM*, 30)—particularly in "Light Shining Out of Darkness" (*AM*, 21– 33)—we really have but one spacious vision that allows connections to emerge without arid intellectualizing.

The Fruit Man, The Meat Man & The Manager

If *Around the Mountain* can be thought of as a cycle of stories spinning about the emblem of the mountain that gives us increased perception, then *The Fruit Man, The Meat Man & The Manager*[26] can be read as a series of panels about grace and penance.

Grace, in Catholic theology, has a trinitarian aspect, and Hood puts us in mind of the Trinity by the very title, which he explains as follows: "The Fruit Man is God proffering the apple, and the Meat Man is Christ incarnate, and the Manager is the Holy Spirit moving the world. The Manager manages the world, the Meat Man offers himself for us to eat, and the Fruit Man places the knowledge of good and evil in the middle of paradise and tells us not to strive too high for it."[27] The title story (*FM*, 188–97) is very much about the economy of grace, which magnifies the God who is present in all men who open themselves to Him.

Hood's story begins with the Greenwood Groceteria run by three partners—Morris Znaimer, the manager; Jack Genovese, the fruit and vegetable man; and Mendel Greenspon, an experienced butcher. Znaimer is the father-figure, a "shrewd judge of credit" (*FM*, 188), and together the trio keep abreast of their competition by "maintaining high standards of goods and services and fast free delivery" (*FM*, 189). The small store cannot really compete against supermarkets, but Znaimer's fatherly look and genial business manner attract customers such as Sarah Cummings. A turning-point is reached when the university next to the store wants the land for a new sports center. The university makes a good offer, and Jack and Mendel want to take it, though Znaimer does not. Since he cannot afford to buy them out and since he cannot talk them into fighting expropriation, he agrees to close the store. The atmosphere changes: "The give and take among the partners had not the familiar ease; the drivers booked off drunk more often. Shirley the cash-girl would talk discontentedly from time to time of quitting" (*FM*, 194). The closing comes on Halloween. The store goes out as a ghost, as it were, with traditional festive displays of pumpkins and black and orange candies in the window.

The haunting mood deepens as even the truck threatens to die, making terrible expiring noises. Znaimer notices how bare and cold the trees look and how steely the sky is: "He was in his own place in this neighbourhood and could not bear to leave. He felt that nothing holy was left in his life" (*FM*, 197). His partners find other jobs; he disappears. But a year later, Sarah Cummings receives a Christmas card from him with a short hand-written message inside expressing his nostalgia and desire to return to business. The poignant ending has a dual significance: it seals the economic defeat of Znaimer, but provides a spiritual consolation both for him and Mrs. Cummings. His goodness is its own reward, spreading love to her heart and providing satisfaction to its benefactor. Znaimer is not obliged to send a card. His free, loving gesture acquires a special virtue. Znaimer had always been the special one of the business trio. Charity with him was a permanent habit, expressed most concretely in his system of credit for customers. This permanent habit signifies "a permanent hold of God in man's very being."[28]

Another benign character in the book is Brother André, an authentic historical person whose sainthood awaits confirmation by the Vatican. Following his inclination toward a mixture of fact and fiction, Hood uses Brother André, a diminutive porter at Montreal's St. Joseph's Oratory, as a real-life emblem in his numinous autobiographical story, "Brother André, Pere Lamarche and My Grandmother Eugénie Blagdon" (FM, 55–71). Brother André's shrine atop the mountain in Montreal provides witness, contrary to the narrator's disbelief, that the "penitential intention" is not dying. Petitioners do, indeed, ascend the oratory on their knees, reciting the rosary sometimes, and this public display of penance is a sign of spiritual humility in an age where religious faith is supposedly in decline. Hood obtains ironic humor by playing off the narrator's adult skepticism against religiosity (FM, 56–57). Yet, it becomes clear that the narrator has never forgotten the strong, ineradicable impression that the little porter, Brother André, made on him the summer of 1937. The bulk of the story (more of a reminiscence than a conventional tale) is concerned with getting "the impression down accurately, for the record" (FM, 58)—another instance of Hood's documentary zeal.

Hood's love of fact informs the story, which is radiant with the name, image, and charity of Brother André. Here, again we have the case of one whose way of life is Christian grace and humility. Although he is obviously a household name with Quebec Catholics and a visitor of special importance to the French Catholics in Toronto, Brother André does not act pontifically. Called upon to rescue Réjeanne Moore from her lapse of faith, he accepts the challenge quietly but decisively, comforting the woman by getting her to repent before he leaves quietly. This gentle, unsensational memoir is shaped in such a way that we observe how a penitent is converted to her true nature by a living saint who is surrounded by "some numinous envelope greater than life" (FM, 71). Hood's purpose is to make us reflect on holiness and saints: "Ignorance and superstition are one thing, and holiness another, which we touch sometimes, rarely, and half-miss. At nine years of age, how could I find the saint in the dying old man? Yet he brought poor Mrs. Moore friendship and hope and peace. Saints. What are saints?" (FM, 71).

The figures of holy men appear with surprising frequency in this book, although their holiness is sometimes false and called into question. In "Cura Pastoralis" (*FM*, 173–87) a young Catholic priest is accused of molesting a seven-year-old girl and suffers qualms of conscience. Graham Greene's whiskey-priest in *The Power and the Glory* or Morley Callaghan's Father Dowling in *Such Is My Beloved* might each have recognized something of himself in Fr. Fitzgibbons, who is given moral support by his ecclesiastical authorities in the struggle to preserve what is good and natural in himself without making his life insupportable or destructive. But the priest's personal salvation is not the true theme; neither is his "puritanical guilt" that begs to be punished. Hood hits on the nature of sin that leaves the soul empty and desolate, and implies that by remaining a priest, young Fr. Fitzgibbons is performing a form of penance that converts the sinner again to himself.

A different holy man appears in the comic "Whos Paying for This Call" (*FM*, 198–207), Hood's version of pop legend where a vulgar secular figure becomes a myth in his own time and mind. Written in the first-person, avant-garde pop style (which is to say, it is indiscreetly liberated from the niceties of punctuation, paragraphing, good grammar, and elegant syntax) the story is a parody of archetypes that have become clichés two years after Bob Dylan's advent as a counterculture hero. The narrator thinks of himself as a poet:

> wrote a long poem in prose about fronds   all the different kinds of fronds   saw a number of pictures by an amateur painter rousseau   full of fucking fronds frightened you to look at them big green things about to grab you   i put in orange peacocks and jokes about orange peacock tea next thing the phrase turned up on a beatles track *Orange Peacock Tea*
>
> words that end in cock are pronounced coe in england as it happens and the reference did me a power of good i had a book come out with that on the cover saying i had invented the phrase i dont suppose i had anybody could have thought of it but i did first then I realized those things i would say in fun were poetry stopped giving my jokes away now people tell me orange peacock tea was one of the significant phrases of the sixties uniting in holy grandeur sex urine pot. (*FM*, 198–99)

The narrator falls victim to the mystique of the idol. His beard gives him authority, especially as he travels the circuit looking "heavenly," posing for a *Life* photographer who wants the idol to act like the pope blessing the multitude. He goes through this ridiculous

charade and even writes a winter poem called "The Snow Pope" with
lines plagiarized from Wallace Stevens. His twisted ethics allow him
to defend such plagiarism ("good poets steal all the time"—(FM,
203), and his instant fame distorts his psyche. He is the center toward which the edges of a superficial world turn, but soon this center
discovers its own hollowness.

A desperate devotee from Tampa, Florida, calls long distance for
advice. At the end of his rope because he is dying from leukemia, the
fan awaits "some word" from the master. The hero, unfortunately,
finds he is no "lord"; he has no miracles. But the special edge of this
anguish is blunted by the narrator's bathos: the first thing to bother
him is not the failure of his thaumaturgy; it's the price of the long-
distance phone call! But out of his whacko worries comes genuine insight: "if you look at it that way you can see that every prayer is a
collect call all these collect calls drifting up out of nowhere for god
to accept the charges" (FM, 207).

His failure to find a healing word for the dying devotee is, ironically, his way to self-redemption. "We ask too much of god," he sees
now after he has played a false god with somebody, depending on
him for "the word of life." The only message he can give is like the
air escaping through a pinhole in his blue kazoo. He resolves to scale
down his ambitions and stop acting so saintly and just be a humble
poet from now on. The essential penitential truth of the story shines
through the comic dialectic of acid despair and pop legend, as the
tale becomes a form of prayer or worship by the end.

Another holy man is Menahem Luboshutz, jilted by his lover, who
moves from the profane to the sacred, changing his appearance and
life-style (FM, 102–18). After his conversion to orthodox piety
(through Jewish ritual), Manny's presence becomes charismatic (FM,
113). He forgives all those who had rejected or mocked him, but his
piety is not a life of passive reflection; he acts by giving "spontaneous
delight" to children and adults.

Manny's reluctance to gloat stands in direct contrast to the feeling
of vengeance and moral superiority in "The Singapore Hotel" (FM,
162–72), where Lew Cutter, always under the dominating shadow of
Dougal Baird, his British banking rival, gets an opportunity to exult
in Baird's eventual failure. Like many others in this book, the story
is constructed like a parable. The main banking floor of Toronto
Branch resembles a cathedral, and its windows, with "a velvet trans-
lucent very light gray" glass, suggest stained glass, "perhaps depict-

ing biblical scenes: Christ welcoming the money-changers to the Temple, the Samaritan paying off the landlord, other commercial scenes" (*FM*, 162). The contrast between Scripture and commerce intensifies as Baird enters the scene, delivering his commandments about banking practices as his employees sit in a semicircle "like disciples arranged around their great teacher" (*FM*, 165). Baird becomes a veritable idol. By contrast, Lew Cutter uses only his common touch to build up a clientele for his branch. But this is precisely the turning-point in the story. Baird disappears from view—we discover later that he has suddenly died alone in a Singapore hotel—and Lew is in the ascendant. Lew cannot control his passionate gloating. His survival and success are rewards for his earlier spiritual self-mortification in Baird's presence. But instead of being purged of bitterness, Cutter has a defiled heart.

Loneliness and neurosis often form the basis for a life of penance. In "Paradise Retained?" (*FM*, 153–61) Lassiter is a parody of the romantic hero—the man of superior talents who is bound to be misunderstood. His name suggests lassitude and physical decline, and he lives in the ultramod apartment complex of Habitat, where he is "cut off from civilization, except those parts of it on display under his window" (*FM*, 153). His neighbors have good manners but offer no camaraderie. His own friends stay away from the site—it is too forbidding—and soon Lassiter begins to live "almost entirely in his imagination." He becomes a creature of habit, much like Hannon of "The Good Tenor Man" (*FM*, 72–87), who follows rituals of clothing, food, and exercise. Like Hannon with his Crispy Crunch, Lassiter eats the same food at the same restaurant. By Labor Day he has eaten eighty-six times, and has had three sausage rolls and two cups of coffee seventy-seven times, at the same snack bar. His Expo familiars are always the same: a tall, slightly fat German with "three smooth tight waves of hair going up the side of his head like stacked frankfurters"; a young Caribbean waitress; a sewing-machine woman, "eternally writing names on (hat) brims" while singing a loud obscene ditty. Lassiter and these familiars form "a trio in a folktale condemned to repeat the same action eternally" (*FM*, 155–56). Where Hannon expends energy in a work of mercy, Lassiter's daily rituals are devitalized and despirited. Lassiter becomes a voyeur, doomed to watch trains or ships, and so grows into a Crusoe on his own island (*FM*, 154).

Lassiter's will diminishes. The Expo grounds, the site for Habitat, become a dying Leviathan (*FM*, 158). November, with its "malarial mists, dampness," and "threatened freeze," emphasizes Lassiter's state of mind (*FM*, 159), and as December wears on frigidly the buildings "crumble visibly." Expo Theatre flakes and peels and takes on the look of a relic from a prehistoric era. It all begins to look like a morbid fantasy, as Lassiter meditates gloomily on the symbolic parallels between Expo and the "complex ceremonials" from a pagan era (*FM*, 160).

Vigor returns to Lassiter only in a pale yellow February, after he has attended divine service in the morning. Expo enjoys "the first warmth of this year's sun," and as Lassiter comes to the place of summer fountains, he has a vision of the whole of Expo '67 rising up in front of him "like the bodies of the Elect at the last trumpet." The decadent island becomes an apocalyptic setting of the dead, not the blessed. Lassiter thinks of all the myths of Camelot, the Blessed Isles, the Great Good Place, and dismisses them with an effort (*FM*, 161).

Lassiter's story is a parable of destruction. A man who is given the means to free himself by enlarging his mind, will, and heart immerses himself in a monstrous setting which denies human commerce and imposes on himself ritual bondage. His setting becomes false and impalpable, as if it were an airy dream, and so it is no surprise when it does tear apart for the inevitable working out of divine justice. There is simply no dispensation for this ritualistic antilife.

Hood's aesthetic complex and synthesis are achieved through a religious approach to life, and here Coleridge serves as an inspiration, for he, like Hood, sees God as the embodiment of a Trinitarian view which "resolves dualities through the creation of a synthesizing Holy Third."[29] The Trinitarian view (fundamentally Catholic rather than purely Coleridgean) dominates Hood's moral vision, which perceives that "unity and trinity are built into existence," and that "life is shot through with Trinitarian structures."[30]

The first three stories are "a deliberately-related triptych" in which, as Hood contends, "human art and love are models of immortality." Each of the three shows a soul-defining struggle within a texture of feelings. "Getting to Williamstown" (*FM*, 9–21), the first one, uses a car journey as its vehicle of omniscient observation. The main character, Harry Fessenden, has a bad heart (though no ill feeling toward others) and lives on borrowed time. His preoccupation—against all advice—is with a journey to Williamstown, and the story filters through his mind and soul. Harry is dying through the story, which ends startlingly inside his coffin. But aside from this gimmick of narration, the story is quite a simple one as we witness internecine family strife over his estate. Harry remains benign to the end, and even in death his spirit remains kindly.

"The Tolstoy Pitch" (*FM*, 22–37) takes an artist as its central figure and shows the pain of his compromise with materialism. Frank Pastore tries to be a "close-mouthed writer" who does his own work and minds his own business, but he gets neurotic in the process, becoming "invisible" in the world. Aware that a writer must care "about the world and the flesh, by definition," he is anguished by his withdrawal and further beset by troubles in the way of materialistic temptation. Hence the title with its literary and commercial allusions—the name of Leo Tolstoy bound in with a sales pitch for vulgar success.

Pastore's dilemma as an artist resembles, as he thinks to himself, the "classical first stage of the religious life, the gradual detachment from sense" (*FM*, 29). He loves his wife, Sandra, his friends, and God. But things are "beginning to melt" on him and "run off the table." He wonders "what has happened to that minute obsessed interest" he used to have in "the details of physical life, skirt lengths, peoples' incomes" (*FM*, 30). In this state of weakened sense and will, he has to make a crucial choice between writing out of large literary ambition so as to end up as good as Tolstoy, or writing simply to make money. His talent is in demand by a film producer, but Pastore is disturbed by the profane suggestions of commercializing a high, serious, "religious" craft. Therefore, the image of "the money changers in the temple" is entirely appropriate to his disturbed conscience (*FM*, 32). Actually, the mixture of Tolstoy and Christ is craftier than is first suggested. It was Tolstoy who wrote explicitly about Christ in his didactic tracts and stories, and Tolstoy, like Christ, used the parable to entertain and instruct. Now Hood's story takes on the form of a parable as it follows Pastore's desire to "affect the attitudes of a great and simple man, precisely what Tolstoy did," without falling victim to the delusion that he is either a saint or a great artist (*FM*, 34).

The film producer has a story which he wants Pastore to expand into a novel so that the book can be sold to the movies on the basis of Pastore's name. Hood's emblem of this temptation is an analogy Pastore draws with a Huckleberry Hound cartoon in which the character grows BIGGER AND BIGGER AND BIGGER (*FM*, 33). In actuality,

Pastore feels diminished as a craftsman—though he well knows that it is no sin to want to make money. In the end, he accepts the producer's proposition (the story idea sounds oddly *Russian* to Pastore) and is praised for being "a real pro, sincere, and a great guy" (*FM*, 37). The upshot, of course, is that Pastore is professional but not sincere. He compromises to save his hide and fails to magnify his soul as an artist.

The third part of the triptych is "The Solitary Ewe" (*FM*, 38–54), which Patricia Morley characterizes as having "a recurring mood, almost a hallmark (Hoodmark?)" of "a funny-sad feeling, a combination of humour with irony and pathos."[31] This story is about a romantic triangle. Peter, a McGill graduate, "handsome and well fed," always has "the look of one whom the gods had blessed with every gift, intelligence, health, modest wealth, a clear conscience" (*FM*, 38). He has his own very popular TV show in Montreal and enjoys a healthy reputation as a media celebrity. He is the type who equates love with "the glands and glandular secretions" (*FM*, 40). His friend Charlie, on the other hand, scorns love as an idea from nineteenth-century novels (*FM*, 40). As it develops, the two fall in love with the same woman, Janine, who works for International Service. Charlie comes to experience love and discovers to his amazement that the feeling is, indeed, mysterious—not especially sexual or painful or quasi-religious, and very difficult to specify (*FM*, 47). But it is Peter who appears to win Janine because he is expert in selling himself, as Charlie is not. So Charlie, at the height of desperate anger and disillusioned by "lies all around us," vows to fight for what he wants—the love of a woman. The scoffer is scoffed at by fate, and is up against high odds.

The Fruit Man, The Meat Man & The Manager skirts the banal before leaping to larger matters. Sentiment and wit are always in good supply, whether Hood is being merely playful ("The Dog Explosion"—*FM*, 143–52), keenly sensitive to voice and motivation ("Harley Talking," "Whos Paying for this Call," "Cura Pastoralis"—*FM*, 133–42, 198–207, 173–87), or technically experimental ("Places I've Never Been"—*FM*, 88–101). The impressive range shows Hood's continuing attempt, as William New puts it, "to reach from the known to the unknown" and to explore "the unanswerable paradoxes of human behaviour."[32]

Hood's mind never sleeps, yet it has a controlled dynamism rather than an anarchic restlessness. It always conjures up an essentially religious fiction without being solemn or ramified to the *n*th degree. In spite of its meditative cast, this mind does not suppress the ecstasies of the senses.

Dark Glasses

Dark Glasses[33] is probably Hood's most meditative collection, for it examines characters who fight spiritual battles against fear, guilt, deception, and other imperfections. Taking as its guiding text a quotation from St. Paul to the Corinthians, *Dark Glasses* is about the difficulties of seeing into the nature and truth of reality. "For now we see through a glass darkly; but then face to face" (1 Cor. 13:12). St. Paul's text is fraught with significance, for it touches on three important allied things: vision, the imperfection of human knowledge, and prophecy. Hood's twelve stories coalesce around two of these themes and derive most of their force from qualities of light and disguise. They are arranged so that they begin with problems of penetrating disguises and paradoxes of matter and end with an allegory of man's fate.

The first story, "Going Out as a Ghost" (*DG,* 7–21), is a Halloween story that starts in the "sombre mysterious end of October" when children adopt comic and archaic disguises (*DG,* 7). The central figure is a family man who jokes about going out as a ghost—the most facile, clichéd, and unimaginative mode of Halloween disguise, "the lowest deep of impoverished fantasy" (*DG,* 7). Yet this impoverished fantasy transforms itself. We have a hint of this in the gorilla-mask in his children's collection. The father is troubled by "the human cast of the bestial shape" (*DG,* 8) and has special reason to be so troubled when he is forced into the fate of a former school acquaintance, Philly White, a con-artist of the first degree.

Philly White, detained at the Centre de Prévention, a quasi-jail, makes a ghostly appearance as a disembodied voice on the telephone. At first, the protagonist thinks this melodious voice sounds familiar, but then finds it wholly unrecognizable. The mood of uncertainty is compounded by the air of mystery and deception surrounding Philly White. To begin with, White is convicted of fraud but continually lies about many things. The detention center is a glass building that is called "deceptive" and "the embodiment of a lie" (*DG,* 11). White's lies blacken his own reputation and are an ironic counterpoint to his surname and white complexion (*DG,* 11).

The protagonist does not want any responsibility for White or any role in the man's life, but Philly White will not simply go away or dematerialize. He keeps phoning his unwilling "friend" and lying on and on about his life. When the protagonist finally spurns White's last phone-call and then receives a young Halloween visitor dressed up as a ghost, he wonders about the morality of his action, and we wonder, in turn, who the real ghost is.

Lawrence Mathews argues:

> . . . the protagonist's effort to help White can be interpreted as an attempt to go out as the Holy Ghost, to affect White's life in a way analogous to the way in which the Holy Spirit changes the lives of the Christians in Acts 2. The protagonist can, to some extent, be associated with the Holy Ghost as the continuous presence of God in this world; but he also fails to personify the Holy Ghost successfully, fails to embody the unlimited outpouring of love signified by the feast of Pentecost, and withholds part of his humanity from White.[34]

Reality sometimes costs us a vital part of our humanity. In "Socks" (*DG,* 22–28) the Calabrian immigrant Domenico Lercaro tries to take control of his new life in Canada, away from the "unchanging metallic sky, crazily turbulent weather, an everlasting feeling of being at the edge of the world" (*DG,* 22).

The twin story, "Boots" (*DG,* 29–35), with its wry tongue-in-cheek humor, is about a married woman's stubborn fight against the tyrannical politics of fashion. Her battle is essentially a moral one against the immorality of popular fashion, and transcends purely chauvinistic elements.

In *Dark Glasses,* Hood's brilliance is never obtained by contrived glamour or brittle cleverness. The prose has a hard glitter, and the wit pays homage to man's ingenuity without ugly cold pride. Apparently unable to write a boring paragraph, Hood successfully mediates between the secular and the sacral, keeping his characters intensely human while probing their souls with deft sensitivity and delicacy.

In "Thanksgiving: Between Junetown and Caintown" (*DG,* 63–75) Hood shows us how to transform what could easily emerge as a merely chauvinistic story of a woman's scorn for her husband's "pathetic dependence on what people tell him" (*DG,* 63) into a tropological story of subtle tremors. On the surface, the story is a contest between male and female. It opens with an image of a hill shaped like a female breast and ends with an image of a boar's testicles.

As husband and wife lose their way during a hill-climbing adventure, the wife panics and becomes resentful, but the cheerful husband becomes full of ideas and advice. They arrive at a pig farm in Junetown, where they find an enormous boar glaring balefully from "a stinking square of fenced dirt" (*DG,* 74). After a thanksgiving meal in a farmhouse along the Caintown road, they drive homeward with the wife silent instead of thankful for her husband's intelligence and cheer.

As Lawrence Mathews points out, the story links the secular and the sacral. He points to Hood's use of the names "Junetown" and "Caintown"—"Junetown having unmistakable overtones of Eden after the Fall, especially when set beside a town named after the first murderer"[35]—and Mathews shows how the husband is the woman's savior. The narrator's meditation on "personal incapacity" (*DG,* 69) becomes a metaphor for spirtual lapse, "an identification which Hood reinforces by describing the narrator's subsequent experience in terms of being lost (itself a conventional image of alienation from God) and fearing death (which, traditionally, came into the world as a result of the Fall)."[36] The pig farm, with its "stinking square of fenced dirt" at "a crossroads," is their earth, their dwelling-place after their descent, and the crossroads become an emblem of their crossed positions of power and grace. What Mathews fails to see is that although the wife is not as "dreadful" as she once was, she is still mean-spirited because, in failing to give thanks on Thanksgiving, she becomes symbolically a child of Cain—a creature incapable of ending her feelings of rivalry that ultimately close off her ranges of action and freedom.

Many of the stories in *Dark Glasses* can be read as panels in an allegorical sequence of virtues and vices. To the themes of justice, fear, contempt, and dependency, which we have already seen, we can add themes of guilt ("Incendiaries"—*DG,* 53–62) and ambition ("The Pitcher"—*DG,* 97–109). Yet, none has the philosophic tenor and comic tone of "The Hole" (*DG,* 110–18), the force of "Dark Glasses" (*DG,* 119–29), or the subtlety of "An Allegory of Man's Fate" (*DG,* 130–43).

In "The Hole," Hood attempts to articulate extremely difficult philosophic paradoxes about matter. The story is about Professor Laidlaw, Waynflete Professor of Mental and Moral Philosophy at a provincial university, who is laid low (even unto death!) as he tries to grapple intellectually with the phenomenology of matter. At the beginning, he is a thinker given completely to wonder and silent meditation in Sam and Kitty's diner, where he looks at the hole in a doughnut to contemplate its meaning. The doughnut hole is Hood's witty way of satirizing the hole in Laidlaw's mind and the problem of the "whole" in philosophy. The deeper he goes into reflection, the closer Laidlaw gets to self-hypnosis or sleep: "There was something powerfully soporific about this kind of speculation: perhaps it was dangerous, and this was nature's warning" (*DG*, 112). So we chuckle at Laidlaw's grave self-absorption and yet take the warning seriously.

Laidlaw goes through various existential states of wonder, doubt, fear, nausea, and perplexity, but these do not divert him from the problem of the impenetrability of matter. By meditating deeply, he puts himself into a state of catalepsy, and Hood's comic exaggeration lampoons all those academics who take their own thought so seriously as to have the world fall away from them. Hood's parody of philosophic reflection (where Laidlaw resembles a bullfrog as he shuts his eyes tight and inflates his chest—*DG*, 115) does not, however, reduce the high seriousness of the philosophic underpinnings. Laidlaw meditates on God, infinity, number, the universe, and causality, in addition to surfaces, space, and matter. But his fundamental problem is not merely the fact that he is grappling with the unknowable; rather, it is the problem of his approach to reality. When he quotes from Carew's lovely, elegant, and witty poem about "the fading rose" (*DG*, 113), he misses the incongruity in the situation of a man trapped in imageless thought yet quoting from a courtier poet who thrived on conceits or highly exaggerated images of reality. It is only as he starts dying that Laidlaw begins to turn thought into imaginative images before succumbing to the phantasm of death:

He began to imagine he'd arrived at an unconditioned sense of pre-existence where he was in his cause, that is, in or annexed to or issuing from or conceived by or held in the Divine Mind, in a state of unmixed creaturehood before locality caught him. Not before birth. More like in the idea of himself in the Creator's eternal contemplation of His Essence.

This was colourless but not invisible or outside the possibility of experience. It was not an annihilation of himself. It was like finally grasping the definition of himself, seeing everything he meant, unconditionally and in an instant.

Outside students came and went, expecting the professor to hand back their papers, neatly graded, but he never did. He wasn't dead, not what you'd call dead precisely. But a lot of people came to somebody's funeral. (*DG*, 118)

Laidlaw's abstract reasoning is gently mocked at the end as, in trying to take on the wholeness of matter and being, he loses the whole of life.

Laidlaw appears to incarnate Descartes's intellectual nominalism when he allows so much to the intellect that conceptual reality becomes his only reality, and his imagination fails to develop. By repeating Carew's verses as an incantation or prayer, Laidlaw tries to banish nausea (*DG,* 113), but, in essence, he is really attempting to lose sensory awareness of his body as he indulges in pure intellection. When his imagination does exercise itself in images, it produces appealing forms that might be products of delirium. The final passages quoted above work out what Berkeley believed was the monism of knowledge—the lack of distinction between inner and outer—and Laidlaw's final "feeling" of reality is the *presence* of the known in the knower as he becomes a ghost.

Pure meditation, then, is not the way to triumph over or cope with reality. Man requires negative capability and persistent faith. This is apparent in "An Allegory of Man's Fate," which has been unwisely dismissed as a "trifle about a suburbanite named Bronson who puts together a do-it-yourself sailboat."[37] Critics like the one just quoted persist in misreading Hood as a literal realist or a satirist rather than an allegorist: "At his best Hood has the eye of a Boswell or Pepys, except that he turns his mania for detail into mild satire instead of the biography or diary of an earlier age."[38] The same critic goes on to state that "the sailboat story is more satire than allegory, certainly, and even Hood's inexhaustible fascination with the *material* of society gives the impression of one who is feeling the fabric for flaws."[39] Now such a comment in attempting to be incisive simply becomes fatuous. Surely it does not require the perception of a genius to notice an allegorical emblem in the sailboat that Bronson is building. It is an ark of his own making, and the entire story, though wonderfully satirical in its illustration of Bronson's marital and avocational tensions, is shaped carefully.

In Hood's mind, boat-building never exists as an act in itself: "If you start thinking about building a boat, you're going to be led to all kinds of scriptural analogies—like the boat on the lake of Gennesaret where Peter says, 'Lord, save me,' or the building of the ark, or the sending out of the dove, all those things—and there's no way to deny or remove that from contemporary writing."[40] Hood brings in associations with Noah's ark, *The Seafarer,* the *Titanic,* and even

The Poseidon Adventure, because "you can't write a story in a vacuum. Any boat story is going to have all these things carried along."[41]

The moral thrust of the story is felt early. Bronson's work begins just after Thanksgiving, and has the benediction of his own optimism: "There is no difficulty that cannot be overcome" (*DG,* 131). Though doubt, frustration, and anger corrupt his soul at times, Bronson holds fast to his belief. Yet his character is not simplified or idealized; there are intimations of *hubris*:

> "It's for all of us," Bronson said. "We'll all have fun building it, and then sailing it." Afterward he wondered if this speech had exhibited the savage, unknowing pride of strength and power called *hubris* by the Greeks—an attitude that delivers punishment in its very structure. (*DG,* 135)

Religious symbolism enters via the ark image and makes its impression through the "mana" of family spirits and folk narratives, and in the "tabernacle" housing the unassembled boat (*DG,* 136). In spring, the family cover the "tabernacle" with a tarpaulin and return to town to "meditate" (*DG,* 136), and so the "actual unveiling" takes place in the summer. The boat-building is a holy task to Bronson, who never loses faith in himself, despite the inadequacy of his technological resources. "I am enlarging my range, confronting and overcoming obstacles; nothing human is alien to me," Bronson thinks. "There is no difficulty that cannot be overcome" (*DG,* 140). The last sentence becomes a refrain, a chant or prayer of hope. Nothing is simple about the boat-building, and Bronson knows that it might take months, possibly years, to complete. But he finds in this fact an analogy for life itself: man's fate is to endure, to go on to the end because existence takes years to round off, to be given a discernible shape (*DG,* 141–42). Difficulties—even in his own marriage—do pass away, and the completed boat is an emblem of man's self housed in the gifts of his own spirit.

The ark in this story points to an important feature in Hood's aesthetic. As J. R. (Tim) Struthers has pointed out, Hood begins with an object and builds the universe or fictional world to which that object belongs.[42] Hood has something of Alice Munro's density, but his range is wider than hers, and his materialism provides a sense of existence where objects serve as structural elements. Cases in point are the old radio in "Where the Myth Touches Us" (*FRK,* 189–217), the documentary movie of the miracle-mile race in "The End of It"

(*FRK,* 218–39), and the picture of W. C. Fields in "Nobody's Going Anywhere!" (*FRK,* 158–75). The details are a transmission of the fullness of life, because particular realities are never merely themselves but are things that set off vibrant radiations of association with even abstract ideas.

Dark Glasses amply demonstrates Hood's metaphysical style where a concern with the physical facts of existence is allied to a metaphoric sense. The most virtuoso writing in this book is in the title story, which links up three main themes—justice, vision, and the impenetrability of reality. It is such a compact story and so craftily constructed that its language of confession brings to light various things that are embedded in a matrix of emotion and reason. Through his revelations of a Jewish couple scrupulously dedicated to the pursuit of social justice, the narrator shows the psychology of the justice-seeker.

Dark Glasses (*DG,* 119–29) is not simply about relative or finite or optimal justice. It is about the psychology of a scrupulous conscience as this alienates the just man from others and, perhaps, ultimately from himself. In this way, it is a complex tropological story. The justice-seeker becomes blind to himself and loses his objectivity and virtue.

The story, we are informed in the opening sentence, comes from "the quality of the light," and it becomes increasingly clear that Hood has St. Paul in mind. It is a mid-February afternoon with "strong sun-glare over snow, a hard-edged Northern Lights dazzle," and the anonymous narrator, a faculty member of a distinguished institution, needs the smoked lenses of his clip-ons (*DG,* 119). He is on his way to a party devoted to "the public life of politics and affairs and institutional art, to intrigue among persons seeking to have their writing published, and avowals of liberal and even radical social ethics on all sides" (*DG,* 120). He feels uneasy about his dark glasses, remembering that psychiatrists consider the wearing of them to be a hostile act (*DG,* 119). He confesses, however, that he likes "manufactured opaqueness" and "swimming deception" (*DG,* 120). His cityscape disguises things the way his smoked lenses tint his vision. As he climbs around Westmount, the houses seem big and bogus, though no less false than the party conversation.

The dark glasses become an intriguing emblem. On the one hand, the protagonist remains apart from the other guests and their phony talk. Yet, he is clearly hostile when he is engaged by a guest in a

brief discussion of his literary work. The sad stories he writes reflect
the vision he has of the world: "Some people are crippled like that
and can only see disfigurement; we smell out hurt the way a dog
traces his quarry. Most days I feel fairly good, but I'm always on the
alert for others' misgivings" (*DG*, 122–23). His brusque comment is
made as his eyes hide behind the dark glasses. This is an impious
moment, a deliberately stiff-necked rebuke to a well-intentioned
guest. But a much bigger shock is yet to come whereby the narrator
is himself defiled and learns the shame of hiding from the course of
things.

He sees a Jewish couple, the Leventhals, whose acts have touched
his life in a significant way. He feels like a son to Herman Leventhal,
a distinguished lawyer and liberal thinker who, like his wife, Yetta,
is a social radical always agitating for justice. It has been some time
since he appeared as a defense witness for Herman Leventhal in an
obscenity trial that fought against censorship, and the narrator knows
that the Leventhals have recently and tragically lost Chaim, their only
son. He moves toward them, revering their courage and persistence,
but meets with a strange reception. The environment takes on a subtle chiaroscuro, but the drama in the room is no less subtle. The Leventhals treat him as a stranger as they engage in a vehement discussion of true socialism. The narrator wonders if he is having an
hallucination, for the couple seem crazily off key to him as the dark
light intensifies around them. Metaphorically, the dark light, as Lawrence Mathews has observed, can be related both to the narrator's own
artistic vision (which sees only sad stories) and to the dark psychological state of the Leventhals. It is Hood's mood of decline, for the
"dark light" suggests Milton's "darkness visible" in Book 1 of *Paradise Lost*.[43]

When the narrator moves to offer the couple his condolences on
their recent bereavement, the husband brushes away the gesture and
continues with his impassioned discourse on social justice. The narrator is shocked beyond belief. Chaim's ghost seems to stand in front
of him, and the Leventhals become a grotesquely shrunken couple
whom the narrator cannot bear to face. He clips on the dark lenses
and hides his eyes, wishing the couple would do the same. He wants
their faces covered up (*DG*, 129).

The Leventhals are people who, in rejecting charity, hide from
God's love. If they are justified in their cold action, the course of
things no longer has much meaning. Their situation is uncomfortably

equivocal. On the one hand, by their total commitment to the idea of social justice they are laudable; on the other hand, their abstraction and detachment from charity render them less worthy of respect. Ironically, their impious brusqueness and vehemence become a form of injustice because they are in exile from love and outside the totality of being.

There is further equivocation, for the narrator is himself culpable. Where the Leventhals are extravagantly zealous of social reform, he hides behind the dark glasses of self-righteousness. Yet we see through his dark glasses the very imperfect heart of man.

None Genuine Without This Signature

In his most recent collection of short fiction,[44] Hood turns to the signatures of our times, whether these be in sports, commerce, media, interpersonal relationships, music, et cetera. This is, perhaps, Hood's most accomplished collection, where the language dances differently from story to story, acquiring additional grace from the signature of Hood's calm, spiritual self.

Several qualities make Hood an exceptional writer of fiction. First, there is a documentary sense that has few contemporary equals. Texture becomes a finely wrought substance obtained basically from an encyclopedic compass of fact. We always know how a particular period or society looks and feels and sounds, because Hood constructs his representations with minute detail and precision. It would be no exaggeration (or hostile criticism, for that matter) to call this skill a cataloging craft.

The story which yields the greatest evidence of this, and to fine satiric effect, is "God Has Manifested Himself Unto Us As Canadian Tire" (*NG*, 1–11), which first appears to be about the consumer society. The title is deliberately profane as it takes mass production of goods to be a form of God's signature of creation and plenitude. The narrator is obsessed with Canadian Tire newspaper advertisements, as is his mistress, Dreamy, who snuggles up beside him on the arm of their Naugahyde recliner:

"I want the eight-ply steel-belted Polyester Radials," she whispers, "with the added protection of Hiway-Biway Winter Big Paws." She leans closer, blows in my ear as I turn the supplement inside out. There's a terrific buy on STP in the centrefold.

"We smoke up? We get a little potted, baby?"

"What have we got?"

"There's this little baggie of Tucumcara Gold, smell it sweetie." She rolls over on top of me and I think: beachballs. (*NG*, 1–2)

This appears to be rather glib satire, but it is effectively cumulative and repercussive, for it unites manners and morals and emphasizes temptations of appetite. Cheap sex and drug usage come in for some digs, but Hood's point appears to be that if appetite is all, there is bound to be a deadening of the senses. His two characters, whose voices show that they are really "types," live in order to consume, but they do not discriminate in their consumption. The male narrator (whose initials, A.O., suggest that he is the Alpha and Omega catalog of all goods) has been so devastatingly conditioned to be a consumer that he sees his mistress as a collage of commercial products: "Dreamy is covered, I think, triple-armour-proofed from head to toe, my Breck girl, my One-a-Day girl, made of necessary iron supplements" (*NG*, 2).

We find that the two had first met in a large shopping plaza—Miracle Mart (what an ironic yoking together of the sacral and the profane!). The two find sex and drug "highs," but they are a sad pair as they sit in bed and watch TV commercials. Taste dies (literally, as when all food tastes "pretty much the same" to A.O.—*NG*, 5) and so does sex ("The bedroom has been like a desert."—*NG*, 8).

Yet at the last, as A.O. listens to a TV hard-sell pitch, and rehearses the clichéd, hip slogans of the 1960s, culminating in the phrase "Keep on truckin'," the colloquial snazziness is given edge by Hood's implication that endurance may yield a richer perception.

The temptations of Mammon are also seen in "February Mama" (*NG*, 118–33), a bittersweet Calypsonian story set in Nevis, whose exotic Caribbean ambience is well suggested. Here the pastoral qualities of Peace Haven Inn and the paradisal feelings of the island are resisted and violated by a middle-aged woman with a hot passion for big business deals. Her husband, Rafe Salvidge (whose surname suggests that he is salvaging peace in his later years), has retired to a resort hotel, and his wife of sixty (who looks and acts much younger) visits him for only six weeks in the year. When she discovers Rafe has composed a banal but attractive calypso with a reggae sound ("February Mama"), she jumps at the chance to convert this wooing song into a gold or platinum record. She, an agent who is all ears when it comes to profit and loss, percentages, and royalties, has a vault instead of a heart. Her materialism corrupts her husband's dream of a paradise, and at the end the story is marked by the image of death, as we see in the shrouded faces that flood Salvidge's mind.

Hood lets us witness how internal changes in society are inevitably reflected in the emergence of new styles in life and art, each with its own evolution, transformation, and apocalypse. In "Crosby" (*NG*, 30–43) Hood, a lifelong fan of the great crooner, shows us how an individual so identifies himself with an idol that his personality and style (mimicry of someone else's genuine signature) are in continual conflict with the restless activity of time and fad.

Though Hood is not an experimentalist in the sense of a John Barth or an Alain Robbe-Grillet or a Jorge Borges, he is not as conservative a writer as many Canadian critics mistakenly believe. Even his thin stories in the book have something peculiar in their form. "New Country" (*NG*, 65–76) is a quest story which unfolds as a car trip in which a middle-aged couple gets lost and meets an abrupt end in unknown territory. The couple's chitchat (and how genuinely ordinary it is) has a wry humor but is not at all touched up for literary effect. The chat centers on physical ailments and the couple enters a ghost town. The tenor of death produces a sudden, though not unpredictable, ending.

Also abrupt but in a less melodramatic way is "A Childhood Incident" (*NG*, 57–64), which is anecdotal but reveals the effects of meddling with someone's trauma. There is at first a smart party-scene feeling that is extended by a game of confessionalism: "Everybody at the party had, or claimed to have, something long-concealed and shameful which they now proposed to confess, some nasty fear, some blockage of self-creation under which they had laboured for long and only now were free to unveil, and so escape" (*NG*, 57). But when pressure is put on one guest, young Kate Lynn, to divulge her secret phobia, we are launched into a tale of shame and guilt that changes the entire cast of the story. Her genuine, nightmarish distress feeds the inane appetities of party gossips, but the quick, malevolent ending is poetic justice.

As a general trend, Hood's endings do not shrink his stories; in fact, they do the opposite. Each story expands, emblems unite, and when the literary form is grasped, a sharper meaning grows for us. Such is the case in "Breaking Off" (*NG*, 12–29), where the title becomes a multiple pun. The setting of Commerce Court ("Commerce" acquires several connotations in the story) creates a pleasantly solid and balanced environment, and the name itself joins the mundane and the courtly. The tall floors of this building are towers of bliss, but there is not much bliss in the plot, which traces an unsatisfactory romance between Emmy Ivey (who is an allegorical figure in her "small cave of fact," the photocopy center—*NG,* 14) and Basil Mossington, her nervous suitor. Once again, Hood obtains sharp satiric effect by yoking together incongruities. Emmy, who is a "phantom of delight" with a golden aureole about her (*NG,* 15) and a "ministering angel" or a Passover messenger (*NG,* 16), is also, more profanely, the "office pet" who has no real moral vocabulary. She is surrounded by caricatures and grotesques such as Daffy Duck (the lisping head of the Finance Department), her talking parrot at home, and the blundering Basil. Both she and her suitor are clinically desexed, and their romance has an hallucinatory quality that breaks off in a disco underworld. Basil is presented as a strange, shadowy vibration, and his silly nervousness is contemptible to Emmy, who, however, is more vulnerable at the end than he is, because while Basil finds a way to profit quite literally from their broken romance (by raffling her birthday ring), Emily is humiliated by the development and entertains only malign visions of violent revenge.

More than a romance breaks off. Emmy's imagination breaks off her ex-lover's limbs. Friendships are sundered. Emmy breaks apart psychologically, and the story delivers motifs of fission and fragmentation. After a painstaking exposition of business bureaucracy, Hood breaks off into a very human tale, and he extends the sense of dislocation and disorientation by displacing two characters (Olive and Les) who, for a while, appear to be central in the story. Hood also shows in Emmy's failure to understand her grandfather that a new society has broken off from an older one. Finally, of course, he breaks off the story with Basil's pragmatic resolution of his ruptured love affair and with Emmy's visions of severed limbs.

Hood's style and diction are admirably modulated according to the demands of a story, and this is really a matter of form emerging from the manifold activities of temperament and curiosity. A writer invokes Proteus rather than Procrustes, and when his style alters, the changes in technique represent what the writer has seen of reality. So technique is not merely a trick or device; it is a mode of representing artistic vision which, in turn, represents the writer's external world.

Hood's experiments with technique come to the fore in three stories. "The Good Listener" (*NG,* 134–44) is a montage of voices, unified by the largely silent but hypnotic figure of the "listener"—a mysterious, ghostly, yet palpable figure who makes no sound (except once) as he fades in and out "like a special effect in a film fantasy" (*NG*, 144), listening to various conversations of human distress. He appears to be the inverse of Coleridge's Ancient Mariner because of his compulsion to listen rather than to unburden himself. He might well be the Christ among us, taking on the sins and sufferings of this world, and he is certainly a compelling force that fosters communion among the living. A confessor figure, he moves from spot to spot, "sweeping other people's minds, drinking up their sorrows, emptying them" (*NG*, 144). However, in one startling passage, we note that the listener fails to work his "miracle" on his own son, who resists unburdening himself of Pinterian pauses and questions (*NG*, 143–44).

"The Good Listener" is practically all voice without images, but even more mannered, though much more substantial, is "Doubles" (*NG*, 167–89), which takes its time to announce its themes and strike its key chords, but those doubled patterns spiral together in ghostly waves of haunting obsessiveness. The story is interested in mysteries of personality—in how different people are joined through the reflections of one man's eyes—but the compendium of enigma, analogy, and duplication makes for a very subtle form that suggests music. The narrator is a musical composer who, in spite of various vicissitudes of fortune, and even when his life twirls into romantic disappointment, never loses a fundamental benevolence. Most of his *récit* strikes deep metaphysical chords that braid like a musical score. The remote setting of the Qu'Appelle Valley in Saskatchewan provides the emblem of a magic valley out of which the narrator has to climb in order to reach the meaning of himself. Nature provides yet another emblem in the extraordinary image of a sun inside a rising moon (*NG*, 170–71).

Everything proceeds in pairs in this story. There are two women—one seen in the eyes of the other—and two men. Their lives intersect and unite at different points, as the narrator struggles to grasp the nature of choice and that of love. But these are, perhaps, more distinct patterns than others in the story, for we also have the serpentine double operation of soul and mind, smugness and confusion.

Four "doubles" assert themselves: the twinning of the women; the shared features of the two men; the difference between outer and inner; and a ghostly immanence of being. At times, the style seems stiff and awkward, only because the narrator is groping his way through experience. His knotty contemplativeness, which tries to sort out the doubling realities, struggles with the mystery of a human being and shows an unabashed negative capability: "You can't express a human person, your own or somebody else's. All you can do is think about it and care about it. Rocks, lions, stars, I can handle those, but a person? You have to accept the mystery" (*NG*, 181–82). At their best, his meditations are like strains of music that round off the story with a poignant coda: "Music is the right medium for me. In music, in a song, you can freely mix vice and bliss. Bliss has a better sound" (*NG*, 189).

Cherished by a former girlfriend, Belle, whose path crosses his repeatedly, his final thoughts echo optimism. He is large-souled, healthy rather than neurotic, capable of seeing one form in another and appreciating the duplications of reality. In these ways, he is blessed and blissful. Rather than waste away in envy and meanness of spirit, he rejoices in Belle's contentment and in the role she played in predicting Flory, his wife, to him. Out of such joyful epiphanies come his musical compositions, and as his mental movements follow the motifs of "doubles," the story's final chords fill his soul with spiritual fulfillment.

The story floats in and out of the mystery of the human person, but in so doing gathers together various notes and measures that develop like a fugue into a suspended disclosure, a delayed resolution. The story, through the meditative opening, takes its time, mixing colors and emotions until we reach not a tediously solemn moral but a crystalline climatic moment. The text's tonality is achieved through the revelation of truth and the coordination of action. There is the same constraint in the gradual order of narrative as there is in the order of melody.

"Gone Three Days" (*NG*, 98–117) is an entirely different experiment that first seems unnecessarily quirky and protracted in diction and onomatopoeia. It is divided mechanically into two parts—the first one being impressions of a severely retarded boy in a world whose brutality and rejection he fears; and the second being a male social worker's account of his attempt to rescue this boy from a life of animal suffering. Except for one or two lapses in diction (words such as "shudder" and "crank" are, perhaps, alien to a severe retard), Hood manages (as well as Faulkner does in *The Sound and the Fury* or *As I Lay Dying*) to suggest the burdens of an inarticulate soul who is struggling to express himself and the strange world. The second section clarifies the entire story and reveals it to be a touching tale of love, but in deliberately dividing his story so mechanically and by placing the boy's inarticulate impressions first, Hood tries his reader's patience and ends up telling the story twice.

As in his previous collections, all the stories have firm textures, but one of the most closely textured stories is "Ghosts at Jarry" (*NG*, 44–56), which is about its narrator's attempts to repossess the past and renounce the large emptiness of a new order. The physical contrasts between "the Big O" (Montreal's spanking new Olympic stadium) and old Jarry Park (the narrator's favorite sports haunt) are really contrasts between old and new dispensations. The narrator blesses the old and curses the new, and his disenchantment with the Big O is built by a preponderance of negatives (*NG*, 45).

Using a radio broadcast, he creates a scenario for himself at the old Jarry Park, inventing an audience, playing baseball games in his head, reminiscing about some eccentric fans ("the Gautama of the bleachers" and the whirling dervish—*NG*, 52). Life at Jarry becomes a surrogate experience, yet superior and mandalic, for the narrator feels at home and integrated with Jarry's environment, especially when he meets a young woman who has also come to the park to recapture old feelings. She is a ghost to him, just as he is to her, and they are joined by other ghosts who exorcise the spirit of the Big O by refusing to take it seriously as a replacement for Jarry. The ghosts of Jarry, then, are the true spirits of place, mind, and heart, and the imaginary baseball scenario with its huge audience is the quantification of form—evidence of an ineradicable signature.

The signature theme culminates in "The Woodcutter's Third Son" (*NG*, 77–97) and "None Genuine Without This Signature" (*NG*, 145–66)—the first a rhetorical exercise in analogy and the second a playful satire. Actually, both stories owe something to fairy tale because in "The Woodcutter's Third Son" the uses of enchantment develop a parable, whereas in "None Genuine Without This Signature" the story unfolds like a dream of awesome, magical success. Both stories also share in Hood's didactic craft and power, with the first one casting a spell of language and wit while the second one is offered to us as a mental movie.

"The Woodcutter's Third Son" is about the testing of a human. The first few pages have an elegant formality in their sophisticated wit and acutely turned syntax as we meet John Flamborough, a man quivering with anxiety about "his green middle-age" (*NG*, 77), but who is preoccupied with ideas of law and justice. He is quite enchanted by Cecy Howard, the daughter of a late chief justice of the provincial supreme court and a rather minxish character who brings up the analogy between myth and life. She introduces him to Bruno Bettelheim's view in *The Uses of Enchantment* that "we rule our lives by our inheritance from folklore, by spell, by conjuration" (*NG,* 82). She goes on to explain that we invent spirits that live in things and, moreover, that we identify with a spirit of some principal, major, or famous character in legend, fairy story, or folktale. Flamborough, who never before in his life had identified with fairy tales, immediately reveals that he is the woodcutter's third son—the prototypical darling, the "spoiled favoured child of fortune" (*NG,* 85), with a "fated, angel-protected career" (*NG,* 90). Luck he certainly possesses: "a cloudlessly happy marriage, a spouse who continued marvellously beautiful and wonderfully loving, freedom from any want or the necessity of the least hope deferred, a promising and extravagantly healthy pair of children, girl and boy, almost every blessing, all this had come true" (*NG,* 89).

Flamborough has always subscribed to biblical analogies, trying to live out their implications, but discovers that he is becoming a perplexed, confused, seeking man. Now the world of religious revelation begins to be displaced by the world of folklore and legend. Flamborough wonders what part of his life is arbitrary, magical, and compulsive, and what is virtuous, graceful, and truly spontaneous. The difficulty is to distinguish the two courses of life via their effects upon the soul. An expert in law with a celebrated book to his credit, Flamborough (like Jeremiah, his favorite Old Testament author) becomes harshly denunciatory of others who know nothing of themselves as individuals or as a group. He seeks a deep source in himself and in the divine nature of what he may or may not do. The man who has "had it all" tests himself by using Cecy as the bait and discovers that he has been trying to operate under two contradictory notions of character. His role-playing, as the woodcutter's third son, has divided his soul and turned him against himself. He's neither a fairy prince nor a pilgrim, and he can not live in his fairy tale any longer for his marriage has gone shaky (his wife is suspicious of Cecy), and Cecy accuses him of smugness—"the homage hypocrisy pays to virtue" (*NG,* 97). He is left like a naked, solitary victim, "shivering in the blast, alone on a withered plain which at its verge began to slope downhill" (*NG,* 97). The final image of a magical transformation occurs in many fairy tales that show a life gone wrong beyond repair, and it also has a biblical connotation of spiritual damnation. Flamborough's real signature is revealed to be smug yet confused, an ornamentation of something corrupt.

It is in his title story that Hood spins a hugely entertaining secular analogy for scripture. "Selling is strange. Human," all right, as the narrator contends (*NG,* 146), but so is religion, which spreads its own propaganda, person to person, offering spiritual consolations and blessings instead of material ones. Harry Felker, the protagonist, is a salesman supreme who has faith in his products and can sell anything because he seems to be dead honest. When he becomes involved in the production of natural fruit syrups at Ma Hislop's boarding-house in Sweet Cream, Manitoba, he puts his sales knowledge to good use, assisted by three "disciples": Ma Hislop; her sensually attractive daughter Peaches; and the raw-boned, trustworthy Bodsworth. Having cast his old samples and fine carrying case into the river, Harry now has to find a new way of selling new products, and he develops incantatory slogans which spread the illusion of a lost Eden miraculously retrieved. The bright colors and tones of the Hislop products are not only aesthetically appealing (like the palette of Bonnard—*NG,* 162), they are also a graceful means of giving identity to the products and consumers. In a theological parody, Harry comments: "We're a real presence this holiday season. And I've always believed in the real presence" (*NG,* 163). In the Michaelmas month of September, his strategy is to persuade a buyer to feel "kind of like self-sacrificing. Mortified" (*NG,* 164). And being a concocter of syrups and lotions gives him an enchanting liturgical or sacerdotal feeling, set off by the pharmacist's three globes with rich colors in a window that suggests an altar (*NG,* 152–53).

The religious analogies are intriguing. Harry's revival of his sales techniques is a new dispensation. It occurs in a town, Sweet Cream, whose name (though in one sense highly sexual slang) suggests paradisal milk and honey. The fragrance of Peaches in the bathtub and the glow of viscous syrup color the mood of nocturnal secrecy in Ma Hislop's house, where Peaches puts her luscious body to use to squeeze fruit into pulp. At first there is the suggestion of forbidden knowledge and faintly corrupt events, but Harry joins Ma Hislop, Peaches, and Bodsworth in attempting to get rich by a sweet sacramental.

The ending is comic because of the nuptials of Peaches and Bodsworth, and the journey eastward of the senior pair, Ma and Harry. We might well wonder if the seniors journey east of Eden, but the general mood is one of bliss.

All these clever religious analogies are not presented crudely. Hood is too good a storyteller to be stiffly academic. He gives his tale erotic touches and something of the exotic intrigue of the *Arabian Nights,* but he never obscures underlayers of hard truth. Finally, what matters in a didactic sense is not the commercial success of Felker and his "disciples," or the comic ending. What is left to tease us is the slogan: "None Genuine Without This Signature." Harry knows that Ma Hislop's name on the labels will be a testament of honesty and integrity to the lotion-buying public who think that they are getting old-fashioned quality for their money. Though there is quality in the Hislop product, there is also an element of deception. Ma Hislop does not affix her real signature in full. She uses a purely commercial likeness. This signature is nongenuine.

Hood's book of twelve stories has an organic form suggested by the numerology and by intrinsic patterns. The final story looks back to the first one, for both take root in commerce and media folklore. Indeed, most of the stories could be grouped as media folktales, for they touch such familiar themes as promotion, pop music, baseball, and salesmanship. Hood's title, a clever jest, makes a claim for the value of his own work, and, in giving us the signatures of our times, Hood does so in a voice that is uniquely his own.

Literary Journalism

The closely textured worlds of his short stories suggest that Hood is a strong journalist whose documentary details are an integrally fertile part of his fiction. Perhaps his penchant for detail comes a little from his intellectual curiosity as a professor (in the Academy of Fact, as it were), but most of it obtains, perhaps, from his affection for the totality of the world—everything from hockey to religion, the Canadian Tire catalog to the art of Bonnard, all literary histories, all trivia. Like James T. Farrell, John Dos Passos, and Theodore Dreiser, he tries to get his facts right, double-checking them in encyclopedias and other reference books, going to old photographs and magazines for the look of a period. Yet, his mass of detail never loses the subtle design in his lovely fabric.

This attention to detail is what makes him a superb journalist whose developed view of the world does not preclude his being creatively surprised. Hood is not self-absorbed in his first-person accounts. His personality, unlike Hemingway's or Mailer's, never arises above his work, and so he is able to renew his creative energy whether he is writing leisurely autobiographical narratives or commissioned pieces. His participation as a character in his own journalism (for example, when he steps on the ice with the legendary Jean Béliveau in Chapter 6 of *Strength Down Centre*[45] for a difficult lesson in the art of ice hockey) is graced by a wry humor that undercuts his own pretensions while magnifying his true subject, which is always someone or something other than himself.

True, Hood has not produced a vast amount of journalism, so there is no justification for placing him in the company of such luminous literary journalists as Naipaul, Mailer, or Diana Trilling, but the quality of his contributions is such that we can say that were he not such a superb writer of fiction, he could turn to a profitable career as an art critic, a sports commentator, or a columnist in *belles-lettres*. His journalism is an extension of his fiction in the sense that it is often about the same themes and landscapes that are developed in his fiction. The Ontario countryside in "Innuit and Catawba" (*GB*, 58–69) and the ravines in "The Governor's Bridge Is Closed" (*GB*, 8–20) are personal heraldic elements that establish emotional and intellectual resonances that echo in such novels as *A New Athens* and *Reservoir Ravine*. His technique of evocation is identical with that in his fiction, for he works up a scene in his imagination by digging out "all the imaginative possibilities in a given landscape" (*GB*, 8). Many of his essays—especially in *Around the Mountain*—are written as short stories. As such, then, he is a superb journalist who can crystallize his perceptions and attitudes by literary craft; and he is a crafty fiction-maker who grows in authenticity by virtue of his technical or factual information, which is never simply a pastiche of isolated facts but an integral part of his "documentary fantasy."[46] Hood's accumulation of detail is an attempt to correlate and authenticate his perspectives, and it is illuminated by his sense of history and metaphysics. It usually produces a finely tuned coordination between individual consciousness and the setting in which history and that consciousness grow increasingly complex.

The only exception is curiously in *Strength Down Centre,* his biography of Jean Béliveau, in which Hood, as participating figure and detached recorder of the statistics and folklore of hockey myth, fails to resolve the tension between fact and narrative voice. He tries to write the biography as an Arthurian romance, but he begins with such dry, tedious reportage and stays so shockingly unaggressive as a participant (except for Chapter 6, where he becomes amusingly and intimately personal) that the load of statistics robs the book of exciting thrust. The journalism wins a laborious victory over the romance.

Hood's journalism is often charged by a high moral sense that shows how his whole imaginative life is connected to the perils and triumphs of reality. "The Governor's Bridge Is Closed" shows that Thomas Wolfe and Heraclitus were both wrong: you can go home again and again, and although reality changes in the flow of time, you can step into the same stream twice or oftener. The synthesizing power of human imagination and its relationship to continuing cultural tradition with an implicit structure of morality make it possible for the individual to experience a significant sense of permanence.

More than this sense of permanence, however, Hood's journalism is energized by a philosophical creed that posits "the perfection of the essences of things—the formal realities that create things as they are in themselves" (GB, 131). Using the examples of Vermeer or Hopper or Joseph Haydn, Hood tries to concentrate on knowable forms and his journalism—whether it is an impressionistic study of Ontario ("Innuit and Catawba"), a record of a tremendous shift in taste ("Circuses and Bread"—GB, 21–34), or a formal study of a designer's art ("Murray Laufer and the Art of Scenic Design"—GB, 113–25)—attempts to capture the "visionary gleam" in all things.

Now this is not to imply that Hood is a noncritical enthusiast of reality. His moral imagination cuts into the perplexing entanglements of Canadian history and defines our cultural deficiencies while remaining optimistic about the Canadian conscience ("Moral Imagination: Canadian Thing"—GB, 87–102). Hood believes, even against much evidence to the contrary, that Canada is a society permeated by Judeo-Christian values, and enlarges this feeling in an essentially religious article, "The Absolute Infant" (GB, 136–44), which repeats Thales of Miletus' dictum "Everything is full of God" (GB, 137) while fortifying this with Blake's view that "Everything that lives is holy" (GB, 144). The entire article reads in retrospect like a preparation for *Reservoir Ravine* because history and eternity are shown to be united in a nativity-redemption narrative which is *always* taking place.

The interplay between Hood's fictional and nonfictional work satisfies his need for a realistic base while releasing him for a superrealistic ontology which posits an inspiration from above that enlightens art and other human endeavor. To project this harmony of realism and transcendentalism, Hood has perfected a metaphysical style whose tone is frequently speculative and metaphoric while being simultaneously precise and involved in fact. In his own voice, Hood projects himself as an accessible writer, the journalist of immediacy, not closed in some obscure or distant literary world, but exultant in his communion with common things that he magically illuminates with uncommon light, particularly through emblems.

Chapter Three
White Figure, White Ground

Because its protagonist is an artist of genius whose vision climaxes in a high technical innovation, and because of the many references to artists such as El Greco, Hopper, Dufy, Picasso, Town, Borduas, Riopelle, Rembrandt, and Soutine, some critics have come to regard Hood's first published novel, *White Figure, White Ground,*[1] as a story about an artist's aesthetic problems. Dennis Duffy, for instance, states that the novel is "about painting and the boundaries of art."[2] John Moss goes further and says that Hood strives "for a vision of the ineffable," but then diminishes this view by exploring chiefly the sexual Urthona triangle in the book.[3] Many critics miss the evident form of this novel—an analogy between art and spiritual illumination, or to put it another way, between art and religion.

Hood himself calls the book a religious allegory or parable.[4] He says that it treats art as a form of religious action, "much like contemplation."[5] The novel is ostensibly a quest story in which a highly talented painter, Alex MacDonald, at age forty goes through what his French Canadian wife, Madeleine, calls a *crise de quarantaine* (*WF,* 75). But this is not simply a psychological problem, although Alex is searching for success, fame, freedom, and the truth about his deceased father. Psychology varnishes the real crisis, which is spiritual and which takes the mode of artistic contemplation. Alex seeks to inherit his dead father's house in Barringford, Nova Scotia. He feels that his two old spinster great-aunts have unjustly inherited the home, and he wants to do justice both to his father's memory and to himself. On the artistic level, Alex wants to experiment with light and color on the Maritime coast.

Alex's art has gaiety, and people like to look at it. It does not have "any frivolous literary associations" but his pictures suggest peacefulness (*WF,* 24–25) and are alive with the human presence. Neither Alex nor his art is glamorous; there is no sensationalism in either, just good values (*WF,* 23), and yet Alex is dissatisfied with his achievements. He wants to find the source of light within a medium itself. Success in this technical problem will liberate him from a deadly metaphysical dualism.

The novel shifts between city and coast, private and public worlds. There is also an ethnic split, for Alex's Scots background is peculiarly puritan and his great-aunts clash with his French Canadian wife. A further duality is obtained in Alex's color symbolism. Although white is the predominant motif, black is also an important color. His father's tragic story merges with his own tale of failure and depression, but his eventual transformation turns the story around. He takes a new route home to Montreal, where his career finds a new life. In spite of his love for Ellen Bridport, his cool virginal cousin, he is really sacramentally in love only with his wife, the vital, clever, sensual Madeleine. Alex completes two sensational paintings, *Light Source #1* and *Light Source #2:* the first one expresses his crises; the second liberates him and offers to do the same for Ellen.

In spite of these dualistic patterns, the book attempts to connect rather than to separate components. Hood has always been opposed to dualism—especially the Cartesian type, which sees the world as "simply a mechanical device" and separates the comprehending intelligence from it.[6] He thinks that "bringing together the spiritual intelligence and the world of the senses and the world of the incarnate is the fundamental task of any thinker whether he's a poet or a theologian."[7] Hood's formal academic work and his fiction are both connected and unified by his conception of imagination and abstraction as being the same power of the soul. His doctoral thesis, "Theories of Imagination in English Thinkers 1650–1790," prepared at the University of Toronto in 1955, was concerned with "the psychology of the imagination, particularly in the seventeenth and eighteenth century, and the views of the imagination which evolved in that period towards the mature thinking of Wordsworth and Coleridge."[8] His background in Aristotle, Aquinas, and Dante showed him that imagination and abstraction were "penetrative and life-enhancing and vitalistic" and that comprehension provided the capacity to rejoice in the nature of things contemplated.[9] So, although an artist seeks vision or apocalypse, it is not really necessary or, indeed, beneficial for him to transcend worldly reality; rather, he must remain rooted in the mundane world and understand it as fully as possible before he can make imaginative or abstract leaps into the numinous.

As an allegorist, Hood is closer to Dante than to Spenser because

"Dantean allegory is very much more able to save this world, and to preserve this world, then Spenserian." Hood finds Spenser "dualistic and Platonist and to have not as substantial an awareness of the fleshly solidity of things" as Dante does.[10]

Hood's allegory in this novel is a scaffolding erected around the number three. When the story opens, Alex is thirty-nine. His father has been dead for three years. Having married at thirty-three, Alex has a wife who is now thirty-three. In Toronto, Alex and his parents "had been a solitary isolated family unit of three" (WF, 45). His relationship with Ellen and his wife forms a triangle, as does his relationship to art, family, and religion. He paints a series entitled Flawed Crystals, 1–24, which can be looked at in multiples of three. The book is divided into three parts (Barringford, Toronto, Montreal), each containing eight chapters. The ternary division strengthens the unity, and shows that life is bound up with numbers, especially with Trinitarian structures. Though the greatest technical contemplations occur in Chapters 4 and 8 of each part, Hood explains that his divisions are not primarily dramatic or psychological but that they come out of much deeper needs for articulation in human consciousness.[11]

The numerology, color symbolism, and didactic thrust against dualism suggest clearly that the book is anything but simple realism, although the pure fiction of the story is engrossing. We have a melodramatic family squabble over property, lurid suggestions of incest, and a sexual triangle. On the comic side, we have satire on old-maid aunts, and on intellectuals and their brittle *soirées*. But the integrity of the novel lies in its ultimate displacement of these concerns so that Hood's true obsession with immanent illumination might emerge with startling force and clarity.

The protagonist's quest is not simply after a material inheritance or artistic success. It is more fundamentally a quest after being that is to be illuminated by hope, joy, and wholeness. In May of 1964, Alex sends a letter to his two spinster great-aunts, Claire and Blanche, in Barringford. They find it aggressive (just as they will later find his apocalyptic painting aggressive), but they marvel at his beautiful signature (WF, 14). Alex writes that he wishes "to make some experiments with the light and color of the coast." He also wishes to see the house in which his father was born, in order to discover why his father was disinherited. The mention of his signature is more subtle than it seems at first, and as the art theme twines with the metaphysical, we discover that Alex wishes to find God's signature in things and in himself.

The first chapter, in introducing the inheritance theme and the art quest, sets the white leitmotif before us. One aunt, the slow one, is named Blanche. She wears a white blouse with enormous brown dots, and the clear white background dazzles (*WF*, 9). Gradually, the white leitmotif strengthens, and we find a special significance for the title, beyond a direct application to Alex's painting *Light Source #1*.

The second chapter swings us back to the hustle of the art world, as we meet Abe Shumsky, owner of Galérie Anéantie (a French term for "annihilation" that is found in Sartre's metaphysics). Abe discusses Alex's art career and the allegorical lines of the novel grow slightly darker.

Chapter 3 is a descent by car, as Alex and his wife work their way "slowly down" and get close to Barringford (*WF*, 25). Three elements predominate in this section: the white leitmotif, masculine imagery, and ghostliness. Alex and Madeleine anticipate White Point— a providential name in Alex's quest. When they do reach the beach, Alex faces it with Madeleine at his side, and the lyrical surge of emotion that attends the water's rush is climaxed by his vision of the "mild, white, beneficent" sea (*WF*, 34). Subtly, white takes on equivocal connotations. Just before the sea vision, Alex reflects: "Nobody is black. Nobody is white either. Look at your skin, Mademoiselle Filion! It's a funny blend of pink, orange, and gray, with a dusty overlay. God, but a really white man would be a frightening thing to see. Ghosts are white" (*WF*, 27). Here Hood, like a number of other writers (such as Poe and Melville), takes white as "a rather mystifying and death-like colour, corpse-like, or bloodless, or the white of a kind of terrifying infinity into which you can disappear."[12]

The second element in this chapter is a masculine sway. As Madeleine rolls one of the car's windows down, air fills the vehicle "with a solid masculine assertive rush" (*WF*, 31). This might seem like a trivial point or a cliché, but Hood earlier on refers to Alex's "masculine line" in art (*WF*, 23), and then goes on in later chapters to reinforce the masculine element. In Chapter 5, Alex speaks to Ellen "with a certain masculine caution" (*WF*, 47). In Chapter 7, in explaining Alex's dependence on her and on women in general, Madeleine assures Ellen that he's "not effeminate . . . he's a very manly man" (*WF*, 78). Yet, Alex feels less of a man by comparison with his deceased father: "He was ten times the man I am" (*WF*, 135). When Madeleine discovers Alex's physical encounter with Ellen, she knows that he will give her an "honest, though a masculine, version" of that incident (*WF*, 182). Now there are also feminine elements in the novel, but Hood's point is clearly more than a simple antithesis of male and female. In looking for the ghost of his father and a new vision of light and color, Alex is unhoused, forked man who seeks the true father, God, the source of all fatherhood and art.

Alex's life has evidently turned ghostly because of its obsessive quest after the missing father and inheritance. But a further ghostliness lies in the condition of Alex's art. A top man technically, Alex experiments with media and texture that lead to a diminution of his usual gaiety. The human element is gradually squeezed out, although Alex well knows that "there will be no painting without human values in the picture. Inhuman painting cannot exist; you can banish the figure, the representation as much as you wish, but you can't get rid of the painter and still have paintings" (*WF*, 35). His experiments with automatic painting are unsettling: "Purple for death, I have no doubt," he comments, "and brown for shit." He reflects: "Maybe I am hagridden by dirt and death, boiling with them underneath, so what? I'm a man. I'm not to be driven. I will not wallow in dung. I will not HAVE death. It insults me; I will resist it and I'll beat it. I WILL BE FREE!" (*WF*, 38). Yet, in entering his white period, Alex falls into mystification.

In Barringford there is "nothing but sand and sea and sky" for Alex to paint (*WF*, 45). Ellen's complexion has a "rose on dead-white effect" (*WF*, 56), and the negative connotation for white offsets Alex's attempt to rid his painting of facile "urban cynicism" (*WF*, 58). The suggestion of death is emphasized by Madeleine's insight into Alex's neurotic anxiety about his artistic quest: "The only way not to be provincial was (like Julien Sorel) to surrender the world. Alex was the only man she'd ever known who just didn't *care* and it was the thing she loved best, no, next best, about him. He was not trying to arrive; but he didn't think he'd arrived. If one ever arrived where Alex hoped to go, one would not be an arriviste. One would be a ghost" (*WF*, 96).

Because the book is a multiple investigation, its tone tends to be meditative. Alex's first-person meditations in Chapters 4 of Parts One and Two and his contemplation in Chapter 4 of Part Three confirm this. The family inheritance and John MacDonald's life and death are important points of investigation for Alex, who thinks there is something ugly and sinister about his family history. His first meetings with his great-aunts and cousin are strained and cool. Though his wife's family give him the sense of "ramified distant relations, of manners shared and subtly modified by successive generations of stories and traditions preserved and aggrandized by their constant retelling" (*WF,* 46), these connections do not ultimately satisfy Alex's need for roots. He feels like the son of an exile (*WF,* 50), and his trip to Barringford reverses his father's journey from town to city. He wants the MacDonald house, but knows his two aunts with their history of fierce protectiveness will fight him over it. Aunt Claire does not feel kinship with Alex. Though she admits he is good and decent, she feels "he has no claim" on her or Blanche (*WF,* 62). But Alex is relentless. He takes the whole issue of inheritance seriously, and is determined to discover who did his father an injury (*WF, 89*).

The struggle between Alex and the aunts makes for murderous melodrama. The aunts have already imprisoned Ellen by trapping her forever in the little town and forbidding her to go anywhere else (*WF,* 91). They will "murder" her psychologically if she does not escape from Barringford, and once they come to hate a person, it is for life. Alex, for his own part, is "killing" himself by his own hate and fear, so he needs to be free of family ghosts and wars as much as Ellen needs to be free of the aunts.

Alex's first exorcism results in the revelation of his father's incestuous love for a cousin. Part Two gives us the dark John MacDonald story as Alex searches for the reason for his father's premature death. Alex's first-person narrative in Chapter 4 recounts the history of his father's aborted banking career, failed restaurant business, collapsed insurance brokerage, and a flimsy string of menial jobs. Alex's recounting idealizes his father's charm, love, and courage, and turns John MacDonald's climb back up into a conversion (*WF,* 134). With a mixture of love and guilt, Alex recalls how his father's bad points folded into his own failures as an art student. In 1949, when his father stops drinking abruptly, Alex starts to drink a great deal (*WF,* 132). Alex's conscience has not stopped bothering him, especially as it remembers the fire one hot summer night in 1957 when Alex's bedding is set ablaze by a cigarette he forgets to extinguish before going to bed in a drunken state. His father puts it out, but Alex resentfully picks a fight and almost kills him. His father dies two years later of a coronary condition, but nobody is certain about what

precisely killed him. Alex is convinced that what killed his father did
not begin and end in 1960; it started in Barringford because "you can
take the boy out of Barringford but you can't take Barringford out of
the boy" (WF, 148). He tries to find "the seeds of his death," the
habits of character that caused his father to wear out like "fatigued
metal" at the age of sixty (WF, 100).

His father's death has given Alex a new perspective on things. It
shows him that "we begin in resentment and end in love, sometimes
when the father is dead" (WF, 195), and it also brings him to the
quick realization that he's "the next man up to bat" (WF, 149),
which means he has acquired a large responsibility. His trip to Barringford is to discover his father's ghost in the house and family, but
it is his art, especially *Light Source #1*, that also carries his father's
spirit, for as Ellen exclaims: "He's there, alive! He's there in your
picture" (WF, 149).

One curious pattern about the novel is that in trying to find his
father in death, Alex becomes a father himself. Madeleine, midwife
to his *oeuvre* (WF, 80), is the warm womb in which Alex's procreative
seed finds fruition. In spite of a sensual encounter with Ellen, Alex
loves his wife passionately. Their frenzied love-making on the beach
is erotic in the extreme, but it mixes a Joycean inner monologue (as
in the Penelope section of *Ulysses*) with an abstraction that prevents
it from becoming an opera of enlarged emotions and exaggerated scenic effects. Their sexual consummation parallels the consummation of
Alex's first great picture, for which Ellen, on the same beach, served
as his inspiration. Ellen, who is "beached" for a lifetime (WF, 183),
becomes his "silent partner during the gestation of his painting"
(WF, 156).

John Moss makes much (perhaps too much) of the incest in this
sexual triangle.[13] Surely Alex's incest is as much in his art as it is in
his love. His paintings turn in on themselves as he tries to make the
medium its own source of illumination. He wonders if a mixture of
gel and white oil will "dry and hold and illuminate itself" (WF, 86).
His technical experiment is analogous to God's power to create light
out of His own Being, and returns us to the whole question of spiritual allegory or parable.

The novel is spotted with scriptural quotations, and almost all of
Alex's reflections on art contain some religious nuance. When he considers the necessary elements in painting, he realizes he has left out
freedom—a subject that is also crucial to his theology (WF, 38).

Then, too, his emblematic colors of white, yellow, red, blue, and green are really liturgical colors (*WF*, 38–39).

When he considers the problem of obtaining a self-illuminating picture, he shows his obsession with light from within, a light rising out of a picture like a halo in Christian iconography, rather than like El Greco's light "driving down from above" (*WF*, 159). Naturally, he realizes that he has no light to give, except the light from a trained artistic eye (*WF*, 159).

Alex's career runs into a major block when he gets stuck on *Light Source #2*. Madeleine worries about the loss of his "divine ease," his "godlike freedom of movement." She suddenly sees that "there exist artists, and not just artists, to whom this godlike freedom of movement is denied—people who can't see instantly, and with pure and utter clarity, the full width and sweep of a moral or artistic situation, people who grope and have to make their slow way, unsure, hesitant" (*WF*, 175). She fears that Alex, who is "on the verge of all the kingdoms of this world," is threatened by "some kind of being" like the devil "starting him in this immediate instant on the road to a bad bad end" (*WF*, 177). This is an echo from Christ's temptation by Satan, and Madeleine is determined to prevent any demonic possession.

The most explicit association between Alex's art and religion occurs when Alex confesses his admiration for Haydn, who, he claims expansively, "had the greatest purely musical intelligence in the history of Europe, probably of the world." Alex especially admires the fact that Haydn "always signed his manuscripts '*Laus Deo*,'" and shares with Haydn the view that "All art is religious if it's any good at all" (*WF*, 209).

Alex here is obviously a mouthpiece for Hood, who is convinced that literature is a secular analogy for scripture. Hood asserts that religious practice, art, and love are the three highest forms of human activity.[14] We noted that the first three stories in *The Fruit Man, The Meat Man & The Manager* form a triptych around the theme of art and love as models of immortality. And when we turn to Hood's biography of Jean Béliveau, we see how even this is a spiritual quest— a modern Grail story in which the last word is "Grail." The last time we see Béliveau, he is holding aloft the Stanley Cup like a "huge silver chalice."[15]

Hood perceives God as the Divine Artist who creates a universe which man is given the freedom and responsibility to inhabit and develop. This very idea appears in the novel via Alex's cosmological meditation on the great chain of being. Everything is relative, especially civilization and the arts, so perhaps Alex's innovations in painting will seem like primitive art to visitors from Planet X in a thousand years. Yet Alex will be proud to have been "a cavepainter," of "a fine, ritual-sacrificial art!" (WF, 222). Renouncing his experiments with antipainting and antilife, he returns to paint flesh and the world. That is why his final black picture, although the obverse of white, contains subtle "wonderful, comical hints of green" (WF, 250). Only Ellen notices the green emblem of nature and hope; the aunts do not see it. To them the blackness is most aggressive, violent, and confusing. It looks like "having what's outside inside." But Ellen knows that the picture could also be read "the other way around," and the green tints are emblems of a divine comedy where earth is joined to heaven. The dizzying waves of light are radiations of the infinite, yet Alex is once again a "flesh man."

Significantly enough, Madeleine is pregnant at this point, and she and Alex receive Holy Communion together on First Friday in October. Husband and wife are thereby united sacramentally and physically, and religion is once again made into an explicit motif. Alex's scriptural quotation for Madeleine ("Thy belly is as a heap of wheat"—WF, 236) aptly shows that he has possessed her physically as much as she has possessed him spiritually. They are one flesh, and she has rescued him from Barringford, the great-aunts, Ellen, and inhuman art. In repossessing him, she has ironically given him freedom to create anew with the sort of joy his art originally had.

The novel has its faults. There are perhaps too many stereotypes in the Maritime geography and the family tensions—the sort that Desmond Pacey checked off in a harsh review—"stiff-lipped old maiden aunts rocking on the veranda of a decaying old house by the sea,— mysterious family feud, . . . and ancestral guilt."[16] There is also the melodramatic conflict of two women over Alex. Sometimes, especially in the sensual passages, there is a lush overripeness in the writing, as Hood strains to unite the allegorical mode with the realistic. But the greatest defect, perhaps, is the gap between Alex's folly and his eventual *anagnorisis*. The artistic problem, which is essentially a spiritual one, requires more than a metaphor to chart its development and resolution. Does it possibly come down to an issue in psychology? Perhaps, for Alex at the end is essentially the same as Alex at the beginning—he is still the artist of joy and hope, although with one very significant difference: he has now done justice to visible and invisible worlds. He does not convince us about his despair for all his squirming on the beach in his period of spiritual devastation, and it is left to his wife to explain his dilemma. In fact, there is too much explanation by Madeleine, who, besides acting as a foil for Alex and Ellen, points up Hood's didacticism all too plainly. Hood drives her too hard.

Nevertheless, the comic form is preserved. The novel begins with satire on the two great-aunts and their shadowy ancestors, proceeds with satire on the art world and a cocktail party that ridicules various "types" among the literati and cultural elite, and ends with Ellen's insightful reaction to Alex's apocalyptic painting. Some of Hood's sharpest satire is obtained in his inspection of egos—especially the vanity of the legendary French poetess Honeybear (widely believed to be a parody of a famous Québecoise writer)—but all this is still surface coloring for the real comedy, which is Hood's vision of a soul inspired and redeemed by grace. At the end, Alex is the triumphant artist, the toast of his society, who has made a leap out of the dark into a world of new light. He has come home, out of exile, and fulfills his promise or potential of art and love. The cocktail party is a confirmation of Alex's having chosen flesh and the world over sterile asceticism. In opening himself to God and the world, Alex now truly experiences "God's plenty"—the term critics come to apply to his art (*WF*, 246).

Chapter Four

The Camera Always Lies

Hood's second novel has much to tell us about movie producers, directors, PR men, lawyers, starlets, costume designers, choreography, and montage, while rehearsing the old clichéd plot of a young actress rising at the expense of an older, fading star. It is very much a tired Hollywood story, with ruthless behind-the-scenes intrigue, cheap gimmickry, vulgar sexploitation, and those deceptive surfaces of reality that the movie-makers want us to see. As its title indicates, this novel is deeply rooted in Hollywood illusion. However, *The Camera Always Lies*[1] is not a realistic exposé of Hollywood any more than it is a psychological investigation of illusion. It has neither Nathanael West's savage apocalypse nor Christopher Isherwood's brittle wit; neither Joan Didion's parched vision nor Evelyn Waugh's acid satire. It is a romantic parable where everything is focused on a conflict between its heroine, a glamorous actress in decline, and her enemies and rivals in the film industry.

Critics greeted this book savagely, calling it "unsubtly blatant" in its weak imitation of Scott Fitzgerald,[2] a "distorted rehash of real life,"[3] and a "thoroughly bad novel."[4] Robert Fulford invented a famous canard by commenting that everything Hood wrote in nonfiction had "a sharp, clear, truthful ring," whereas almost everything he wrote in fiction was "dull, flat and spiritless," when it was not simply "embarrassingly pretentious."[5] But these critics did not examine the novel's form, which helps to make *The Camera Always Lies* far superior to run-of-the-mill entertainment.

The fiction has a tripartite division, entitled "Down There," "Going Down," and "Coming Up." The headlines indicate another familiar pattern in Hood—that of descent and ascent. In this instance, the pattern is especially appropriate because the ascending lines of romance fit the solar myth that is embedded in the fiction. If we could stand back from this novel, we would see correspondences between it and the Orpheus-Eurydice myth, wherein Orpheus crosses a wide body of water, descends into an underworld, and after suspending Eurydice's tortures of the damned, returns the heroine to the upper world. Rose LeClair is the Eurydice figure seeking justice in a demonic world of treachery, lies, and tyranny; and Jean-Pierre Fauré, the French new-wave director, is the Orpheus who crosses the ocean to rescue her from suicidal depression and carry her off with him into sunlight.

The story moves from darkness to daylight, from attempted death to renewed life, from agony to transcendence, and there is, overall, a cyclical movement in the world of phenomena that carries us beyond base desires and instincts to higher aspirations. The setting alternates between dry, dark, murky interiors and sunny exteriors on or near water. Part One begins with "evening light" (*CAL,* 4) as Rose tries to resist at the last minute her cold, clammy slide toward death following an overdose of drugs in her motel, ironically named Cresta Corona. She is in a region past New Canaan (another obvious symbolic name), and her life is sinking with the dark. The next scene (Part Two) is on a rooftop patio outside a branch bank on Santa Monica Boulevard, high enough to show gleams of light coming in off the ocean (*CAL,* 11). This is a scene of "sybaritic nuance," where Bud Horler, "a jockey-sized gnome of a fellow," Danny Lenehan, an Irishman "who dresses like a superior squire," Larry Solomon, a studio lawyer, and Paul Callegarini, a banker, discuss business over exotic rum drinks. The orange and mauve beach umbrellas, false-looking grass, mock lake, and swimsuited girls rotating their hips indecently compose a scene that looks like a pleasure palace of "sun and air" (*CAL,* 12). The solar and sybaritic images are later reinforced, especially in connection with the partners Horler and Lenehan, for we see the "sunburnt" Horler sitting in the cockpit of his big cruising motor-sailer on a "white August afternoon," drowsing gently "river-rimmed by sun" and fingering an "aphrodisiac envelope" of "sexy, almost dirty, pictures" (*CAL,* 37–38). The "Pompeian tone" and emblems of mammon strain after the apocalyptic, but they are clear, emphatic, and comic.

The flashback from motel room to rooftop patio, from April to the previous August, and from evening to afternoon sets in motion the cycle of adventure and revives for us Rose's crucial struggle against the wicked system that wishes to sacrifice her in order to perpetuate itself. Rose (whose name suggests floral freshness and beauty) has tried to kill herself because her career and marriage have failed. The studio has plotted to wreck her fifteen-year marriage to Seth Lincoln in order to attract publicity for its new film, and it uses young, sexy

Charity Ryan to seduce Seth. To add insult to injury, Charity steals
the plaudits for the new film and Rose's career is eclipsed. Part Two
shows us Rose's decline and strains to obtain pathos for her. It delves
into the "hidden" world of deceit, betrayal, and violence and carries
us into the gullet of Leviathan, the whole fallen world of sin and tyranny. Rose is the dying goddess, the former darling of the gods, who
becomes the *pharmakos* or scapegoat. She suffers the tortures of the
damned, and her sad fall, set amid the vulgar comedy of the film
industry, gives us two conflicting lines of tension.

As usual, Hood is careful with his text. Horler's name suggests
"whore" and "hauler," and he is a monster of exploitation. Lenehan,
who handles people ruthlessly, claims one of his uncles was a character in Joyce's *Dubliners* and *Ulysses* (*CAL*, 17). Though like that uncle, a man without honor, this Lenehan is not an Irish parasite. He
dresses "like a superior squire" and is a "picture of gentility," but his
name does read like a play on "lean hand"—the sinister hand of
death. The "smart vulgar jockey's air" of Horler and the "squire" image of Lenehan create intriguing nuances. The horse has traditionally
been associated with virility and sex, as well as with burial rites in
chthonic cults;[6] and as the two men are base "bandits, assassins,
thieves, thugs, murderers, robbers"—according to Rose's ex-husband
(*CAL*, 41)—they are "horses of chaos" who force Rose to be a "horse's
ass" at the disastrous premiere of *Goody Two-Shoes* so that their "stalk-
ing horse," Charity Ryan, will win public favor.

The Los Angeles cityscape is "an inhuman landscape" that is "too
much, too long, too wide, too far. Christmas at the end of the world"
(*CAL*, 84). In one comic scene, Horler can find no locale for a conference with his business associates, so the group drives around in a
labyrinthine hell (*CAL*, 83–84). The symbolic landscape is startling:
"expansive parking lots with straggly yellow lines defacing the sheen
of blacktop, with rickety supermarkets in the distance, insectlike
shoppers darting hither and thither across the immensity of parking
lot" (*CAL*, 84). It is altogether a "mad ride."

Hood alters his lighting and colors to counterpoint good and evil.
As the sun sizzles outside, the movie-makers sit in a dim, dusky,
dusty hall (*CAL*, 46). The black mood prompts director Max Mars's
melodramatic reflection on the murderous nature of film-making: studio heads become "Elizabethan assassins" embroiled in "the dark session of conspiracy" (*CAL*, 74). The penumbral interiors contrast with
technicolored scenes of the hectic movie premiere of *Goody Two-Shoes*.

The colored floodlights and spotlights illuminate Rose's moment of glory before her shattering disgrace. The "peachy-rose light" of the first scene in the film (*CAL,* 106) is emblematic of Rose's benign character, suggesting her associations with flowers and sex. Rose is a color that suits both the cult of virgins and the iconography of sex, for it suggests purity as well as female genitalia. This tint is contrasted with the gray carpet and light of Seth's room. The colors are Proustian as well,[7] and are a natural contrast because the gray is symbolic of the ash, decay, and sterility in Seth's new life. After his divorce from Rose, Seth turns remorseful over a wasted marriage, and his room seems full of "dusty pink and gray light" in which he is framed "stork-like and angry" (*CAL,* 234).

Despite the inflated rhetoric of Part Two, characterization is consistent with the conventions of romance and parable. Rose has various antagonists, but she is a passive heroine who requires a gallant hero. She is almost wholly a wish-fulfillment figure who initially has reputation, wealth, and a happy fifteen-year marriage to a Hollywood star who looks like Henry Fonda and has the same surname as Abraham Lincoln. She has warmth, humanity, and goodness, but these are considered "all too unobtrusive" by Hollywood moguls who would like to see her as "more a bitchy slut" (*CAL,* 26). For them, "sex and money" are "bread and butter," so they push her aside to boost the career of their "Hairbrush" girl, Charity, who at eighteen is a real "comer." Rose and Charity are the antithetical females of romance, with Rose being "the nice one" (*CAL,* 28) and Charity the hot slut who cannot be scrubbed clean to suggest toothbrush sex, girl-next-door sex. Rose dresses like a lady; Charity wears filmy black bras and bikini bottoms, and we can feel the flesh underneath (*CAL,* 39). Rose has a "friendly quality" and the warm, "womblike" voice of Alice Faye (*CAL,* 61), whereas Charity projects the feeling of "Saturday night in a Turkish whorehouse" (*CAL,* 31). The studio puts out publicity shots of Charity with a spear to look as if "she's just rammed it in" (*CAL,* 32). They have to sell her as "a dirty girl," otherwise they would be duplicating Rose (*CAL,* 33), but instead of kidding sex like Monroe and Bardot did, Charity is encouraged to ram it down people's throats (*CAL,* 90). Charity's erotic violence is an inverted Leviathan image, a "gullet" of iniquity, where instead of a monster swallowing a human, the monster is forced down some victim's throat.

We are told of Rose's "valuable intangibles" (*CAL,* 21), but we are shown Charity's sensual flesh. Rose has a star-name; Charity the breasts (*CAL,* 22). Charity is turned into a figure of ridicule: her case is "like a novel proposition in formal theology. Condemnation of the first proponents, eventual withdrawal of the condemnation, the slow winning of acceptance, finally the triumphant definition of the proposition as dogma. Charity would be a glimmer on the horizon, then a meteoric presence, then a glowing fireball, and at last a bright new star, coming into existence like the beginning of a universe" (*CAL,* 35–36). Hood parodies theology as much as he jests at Charity's expense.

The problem with the Rose-Charity contrast is that Charity is much more colorful than Rose, who is a dull protagonist. Rose is too good to be interesting in a story of calculated violence, and her passivity is hardly a virtue in terms of literary intensity. She plays her role exactly as required by a heroine of romance, but this role is flatly virtuous. As Charity remarks uncharitably: "Everybody says she's so sweet, you get sick of hearing that" (*CAL,* 57). Indeed, Rose mocks herself: "I'm the letter 'W' in fact. Witty, wise, wonderful, womblike" (*CAL,* 61). On screen, she is stereotyped as an ingenue or in "Myrtle in her kirtle" roles in King Arthur–type epics (*CAL,* 145).

Charity, on the other hand, is rapacious. Pushed by an aggressive mother and conniving studio bosses, she becomes a sexpot, a sex object for male fantasies, and not the authentic person she really wants to be. Ironically, though she loathes Rose's goody-goody image, Charity is so ashamed of her own immodest image that she yearns for respectability (*CAL,* 58). Thus, she is a victim herself.

Most of the Hollywood bigshots personify the demonic aspect of the romance. Faier uses sex to market films; Vogelsang (a cold cruel name!) is an American who sells violence on film. And in addition to Horler, Lenehan, and Solomon, we have Callegarini, who turns the tables on the corporate con-men by bugging their important conversation at the opening of Part Two. The electronic trap fortifies the Leviathan image because the eavesdropping device is a mechanical monster, a man-in-the-machine evil. The studio bosses are compared to Nazis because of their tyranny and rank brutality (*CAL,* 87), and to killers by Max Mars, the German director who worked with Murnau and Lang in the 1920s (*CAL,* 75). Peggi Starr, Rose's trusted friend, calls them "little Hitlers who think sex is a matter of big tits" (*CAL,* 229).

Even Mars, with his dry, witty gravity, is not without his evil.

His films have become less spontaneous, and he is party to Rose's humiliation at the screening of the first footage of *Goody Two-Shoes*. He is now a decadent, his cinema having become destructive and ever more dishonest. In a floridly melodramatic examination of conscience he sees the evil in film-making:

> Max thought: making movies is like that. It takes place in secrecy and darkness and is all illusion. The real moviemaking is when you sit in the dark and change the natural order of things by cutting and juxtaposing unrelated actions. It has nothing to do with real people who suffer. It is an art of excision and splice, like surgery or butchery, with the sadistic psychopathology of those arts, and with the incidental murderous blood. (*CAL*, 73)

This violent mood is intensified in the last three chapters of Part Two, where we witness Rose's descent. Rose sinks into her *agon* and elicits our pathos. Her physical deterioration is marked by inept choreography and a few layers of body fat, but it is accompanied by a crushing sense of shame and a loss of will to live. Her happy marriage shattered, her acting reputation savaged, she is a piteous, doomed figure. Eddie Blanda, the publicity man, passes her and averts his eyes "the way you cover your head at the end of some Greek tragedy or other, as a ritual act of pity" (*CAL*, 121). Once again Hood strains for effect. Pity, however, is certainly what Rose deserves for "the injustice of her situation" (*CAL*, 81). She has no legal recourse, and moves into a limbo with her "death-struggle" at Madame Sylvie's and Goulmoujian's gym (*CAL*, 135). The sadomasochistic equipment—"rollers, surrealistic in conception, straight out of Kafka's penal colony" (*CAL*, 143)—is another physical agony, accentuated by her *sparagmos* or mutilation as a scapegoat. The reducing machine gives her "one hell of a pinch" that goes through her body "like a knife wound." She suffers an "angry red welt" that becomes her ineradicable stigma (*CAL*, 143–45), and this mark, plus the savage wound she has sustained from her divorce, with "her adult life ripped out of her" from Seth's "terrible thrust" (*CAL*, 82), render her a sacrificial victim in a ritual of suffering. When she resorts to sleeping pills and tranquilizers, her body chemistry is deranged, and Rose becomes increasingly isolated from the solace of others. She nearly epitomizes the fate of the darlings of the gods, those who die young (*CAL*, 168).

Yet Rose does not will her own destruction. She hates sedatives (*CAL*, 174), and, as the doctor attests, "she's terribly strong; her organism is not death-centered, but full of life" (*CAL*, 173). That is why her death-struggle in the motel room shows her attempting to reach the telephone and call for last-minute help. But the doctor's pathological analysis is trite and does not do much to make her any more interesting or worthy of tragic feeling, because she has no anarchy in her background—none of the disturbingly irrational forces that so marked a Marilyn Monroe or a Vivien Leigh. Rose is too benevolent to be tragic; we expect her to find salvation because her only ostensible desires are good health, a well-adjusted career, and a happy marriage. As a romantic protagonist she is a mere convention, and as a realistic character she is bland and thin, virtuous but not complex. To an era dominated by Jane Fonda, Julie Christie, and Vanessa Redgrave, she seems quaintly incongruous and old-fashioned. She lacks gall, and soft sentimentality is her dominant quality, as indicated by the deathlessly schmaltzy dialogue (borrowed from an old movie) that she exchanges with Peggi (*CAL*, 174). Only in her showdown with Horler and Lenehan over her movie contract does she show any anger or bitterness, but here, too, she is not as fierce as a woman in her position might have a right to be.

One of the characteristics of such a romantic heroine in her *agon* is that she can be tyrannized by some trait that makes her repeat a certain line of conduct mechanically, and Fauré is afraid that Rose might repeat her attempt at suicide. But Fauré's fear is balanced against a conviction that a person can be sprung free long after he has decided his life is over (*CAL*, 202). Fauré, therefore, tries to keep Rose from settling onto a path that might prove destructive. He converts her to a belief in herself as an actress and woman, and his love for her is translated into a movie offer and a marriage proposal. Fittingly enough, their movie together is to be called *Les Honnêtes Gens,* which Peggi translates as *Decent People* (*CAL*, 222). The montage is planned to reveal the mores of contemporary society and to validate the biblical proverb: "Those that live by the sword shall perish by the sword"—a proverb quoted by Peggi to Charity (*CAL*, 76), and one which forms the crux of Hood's parable.

Violence and deceit run like a relentless dark undercurrent in this novel. Dan Lenehan's idea of life is of "perpetual war, where you screw others before they screw you" (*CAL*, 218). His New York conference room, shared with Bud Horler, is badly lit and carries an "aura of trickiness and half-offered bribery" (*CAL*, 227). The producers bully Rose, are double-crossed by Callegarini, and then challenged successfully by Rose. Seth and Charity wound Rose, but both suffer in turn. The big city is "dangerous," as Hood says in his final sentence, and Peggi, a "pretty, plump, good-natured woman" (*CAL*, 149), is threatened with blacklisting by Horler and Lenehan, who need a target for their rage after Rose's moral victory. Peggi becomes the "somebody left behind" of romance (*CAL*, 202), an inferior kind of scapegoat. Charity foreshadows another ritualistic sacrifice because she is a "fresh-faced heifer" that can be slaughtered by ruthless manipulators in Hollywood (*CAL*, 236).

The ending of the book adheres to the conventions of romance. When Rose is rescued by Fauré and flies off to France to marry him and begin a new film career, some critics take this as a slick, cynical diversion. Dennis Duffy is perhaps representative of this group when he sees this ending as an expression of the inevitable "hollow values of the world Rose makes her living in." Duffy is of the opinion that "the best she can hope for is a cleaner version of the game she must play."[8] But Duffy and others forget that the quest-romance is "the search of the libido or desiring self for a fulfilment that will deliver it from the anxieties of reality but will still contain that reality."[9] Delivered from the violence of the American film industry, and redeemed from her stigma by her gallant hero, she is able to maintain her own integrity against the assault of experience. Her film project with Fauré is to be about the victim at the core of social violence, so it will be a criticism of reality rather than a continuation of its corruptions. Fauré, after all, is not an average film-maker. He is identified as the producer who owns Films Vinteuil. Vinteuil is the composer in Proust who represents "the quintessence of the composer's art,"[10] and Fauré has worked with Renoir, written for *Cahiers du Cinema*, and known Bazin, but is now tired of making coterie films for the art-house circuit. Hollywood movies (such as *King Kong* and *Kiss Me, Stupid*) show him who the monster is in life, and his own meditations teach him how to treat horror in life. He faces all the overt and latent violence in American society and in himself, and is prepared to show others through his own films what madness taints them.

For all its evident merits, *The Camera Always Lies* is a textbook romance that lends itself to scrutiny without the pleasures of sudden, daring leaps out of convention. Everything about it is mechanically contrived, and although the documentary facts are skillfully delivered—such as Jasper St. John's "miraculous" choreography that con-

ceals Rose's weak dancing, or Madame Sylvie's *corsetière* trick of disguising Rose's short-waistedness—the novel never breathes on its
own. Hood pumps the parable for all it is worth, scoring points like
a diligent author who knows his literary conventions inside-out, but
the sophisticated patterns are all imposed from without and do not
seem to grow from within the characters or their situations.

The names are ingenious. Rose LeClair is the not-too-clear-sighted
one who loses her fragrant vitality before blossoming again one May;
Seth Lincoln's names are from the Bible and American history; Peggi
Starr is both aspiring starlet and bland foil to Rose; Horler is a vulgar
merchant of deceit; Fauré makes forays; Charity deserves some of our
charity; Jasper St. John works "miracles" of choreography; and so on.
But such a gimmick, although derived from Rabelais, Defoe, Bun-
yan, Fielding, and Richardson, does nothing to foster autonomy. The
characters are set in the context of a body of expectations, and show
Hood's method of presenting a character as someone whose proper
names are an expression of particular qualities as these are related to
universals.

Even the time scheme is ingenious. The disastrous movie is set up
on a sunny April day, and Rose attempts suicide the next April. Rose
sinks on Easter but is restored to life in May. The summer pastoral
of June and July—Rose and Fauré's excursions into the Connecticut
countryside—extends into the danger of "high summer" in August
when Rose, it is feared, might repeat her attempt at suicide.

Every device is correct according to the norms of romance. The ar-
chaizing tendency (where the inane lyrics and hackneyed plot of *Goody
Two-Shoes* suggest the films of the 1930s, and where Peggi sees Rose's
farewell unfolding like a silent movie) finds its justification in romance's "extraordinarily persistent nostalgia."[11] The musical-comedy
world gives us illusion, music, and craft-magic above the ordinary
world, and Hood's tripartite division imitates the threefold structure
of romance.

But there is a telling strain at the core, and not simply in the self-
indulgently humorous cross-references to Hood's other works, where
Seth is seen reading *Around the Mountain, (CAL,* 63) or where an Alex
MacDonald oil painting turns up (*CAL,* 79). There is a much more
fundamental defect. Hood binds his own values so deeply with those
of his hero and heroine that the characters often become mere mouthpieces for him. Fauré ranks sex, religion, and art as the three most
important things (*CAL,* 98), recalling Alex in *White Figure, White*

Ground. Fauré offers us a very Catholic view of love and marriage as a sacramental union (*CAL,* 97–98), and it is difficult to believe in him as a new-wave film director because he sounds too much like Hood himself in his "consuming ambition to use the medium properly" or in his genius filtering through a "rested and restful" personality.

Everything comes down, though, to Rose. Though she suffers, she is generally too much of a goody-goody to be tragic. Her inarticulateness and orgiastic joy (*CAL,* 212) compound the problem of her uncomplicated innocence. In some ways she is the type of parabolic character Morley Callaghan might have created if he had more craft. But she never takes us down to the depths of irrational suffering. She becomes a sugarcoated heroine—perhaps a lie about the vindication of goodness.

Chapter Five
A Game of Touch

According to Patricia Morley, *A Game of Touch*[1] is "a modern version of the picaresque novel,"[2] and Jake Price, the protagonist, is an artist who acquires a social and political education in bilingual Montreal, where he becomes his society's litmus paper, turning "pink for real people and blue for phonies" (*GT*, 187). But this is hardly a valid assertion. For one thing, Jake, for all his failings and pranks, is no real rogue, and the novel has neither the expansive locales of picaresque fiction, nor the cynical, ironic, or aggressive tones usually applied to a roguish character. For another, Jake is no true artist. Before his bungled graphics for Bill de Zuylen's *Janus* magazine (where he uses the wrong glue and ruins the layout), his only connection with art is a political cartoon he had done as a schoolboy of the schoolboard chairman in his wheelchair chasing the principal down the hall. The cartoon had caused Jake to be expelled after a scene that he turns into a parody of the McCarthy witchhunt (*GT*, 18). Compared to the others in his Montreal circle of companions, he is "just an out of work fake" (*GT*, 32). As a political cartoonist he does not know anything about politics (*GT*, 19). Even his studio is a deception, for he comments wryly: "For somebody who was really painting seriously it would have been a paradise" (*GT*, 30), clearly implying that he does not paint seriously. As an artist, then, he is a *poseur* without any special gifts, and as a rogue he is merely a set of dichotomies with his fakery struggling against his innocence, and his low cunning offset by naiveté and error.

Although Hood gives almost half of his twenty-four chapters to Jake's speaking voice, the novel is not centered wholly on Jake. *A Game of Touch* is a triptych, according to Hood, with a triple theme dealing with "sexual games, politics, and football, all of which are carried on along the two levels, the fantastic and the realistic."[3] The realistic mode, however, predominates.

The novel moves back and forth from Jake's first-person recountings to several third-person narratives, and the twenty-four parts or episodes (each named after a character) begin and end with Jake. The surface is very ordinary. We first see Jake on a long road by which he is heading for Montreal "to have a look around" (*GT,* 1). He is relaxed because he has all the time in the world and does not think he is "going any place special" (*GT,* 5). Although he is twenty, he is merely a small-town boy interested in the big city, and his amiable, low-keyed personality generates little tension at this point. After having hitched a ride to the city, he is drawn into an impromptu game of touch football in a public park, although he still feels like a stranger. In telling the players his name, he converts "John" to "Jake" because it sounds closer to his boyhood name of "Jackie" and because it sounds tougher and more grown up (*GT,* 8–9). This nominal game is counterpointed by the lighthearted rivalry of the two "clowns," Mel Goldberg and Abie Ash, who laugh and horse around and act "funny as hell" (*GT,* 11). Touch football is used as a metaphor for contact, and to exercise some of the tensions of the plot. Hood believes that "the metaphor of a game of touch applies perfectly to so much of Canadian life that most readers of the novel have responded to it at once."[4]

The camaraderie of the first game of touch is extended by a tavern visit where we are introduced at greater length to the various principals and the thematic triptych. The group is like a cosmopolitan cross-section of urbanites, and this point is emphasized by Roger Talbot, a wealthy, brilliant economist of mixed English and French parentage: "I play with Jews, *anglophones,* an artist of a kind, a poet, another professor. A cross-section of opinion . . . and I learn" (*GT,* 36). This is human contact where all sides meet, touch, and learn from one another, even if they ultimately diverge because of differences in temperaments, values, or beliefs.

Although play and leisure are fun, they have a serious underside when they become analogies of life, and Hood uses sport and sex as his principal metaphors of personality and conduct, just as Mordecai Richler was to do later in the hilarious Hampstead Heath baseball game in *St. Urbain's Horseman.* Hood is less uproariously funny than Richler, but no less acute in his exposure of character. *A Game of Touch* is Hood's most psychological novel, concentrating as it does on people trying to find their places in society. Duncan McCallum is most explicitly related to the psychological because he has an M.A. in psychology, with a specialization in testing and personnel assessment. As Jake says of him: "He'd sit for hours talking to you, trying to figure out what things meant or why people said what they did.

Of course he was trained as a psychologist, but he was also very determined to get at the truth of things" (*GT*, 27). Duncan works with
the help of Yvonne Breton on programs designed to evaluate personnel. Hood obtains satiric humor from Duncan's toleration-aggression
scale as Duncan and Yvonne exchange evaluations of each other (he is
T6-A9 by her rating, and she is T4-A7 by his). Duncan is most concerned with Roger Talbot, who is his rival for Marie-Ange's favor,
and with Jake, who resists Duncan's facile psychological categories.

Hood, who usually divorces himself from psychological realism,
here does stay with its norms, although he does not fall into a rigid
grid. Duncan, the arch "mechanical-perfection man," has to admit
that there is no laboratory definition for people because they "act on
their feelings without a definition" (*GT*, 46). People can fluctuate—
as Marie-Ange, Roger, and Jake prove. Roger runs from T10-A5 to
T9-A6; Marie-Ange is T2-A9 when she is with someone other than
Duncan, and T8-A6 when she is in bed with him; and Jake stymies
Duncan altogether, who describes him this way: "Artist's psychology,
tendency to self-dramatization, sees fact in symbolic terms (is a liar),
and nevertheless a disturbingly high competence factor. One of these
people who always falls on his feet" (*GT*, 47).

In focusing on Jake and Roger, Hood deliberately leaves many of
the other twelve characters sketchy, drawing them broadly and
quickly like psychological humors rather than as rounded minor figures. There are, for example, Marie-Ange, the former Angela Robinson from Stoverville, who sleeps her way to biculturalism; Mel Goldberg, the best Africanist in Canada; Abie Ash, who calls himself a
poet; Chris Holt, who comes on like "Gary Gang-Bang"; and Matt
Kinsley, who invents a special grammar for drunkenness. But Jake is
the psychological center—just as Roger is the political one—and he
is certainly not simple to figure out. On one level, he is simply a
young, immature drifter, expecting to live off others. But he has a
conscience to go with his deficiencies and naiveté, and his laziness
and inefficiency are generally innocuous. He is a small-town boy, living deeply in the shadow of Stoverville puritanism. He has heard of
the sexual revolution, but he can not find it except in Marie-Ange
and then only in an orgiastic body-painting session (*GT*, 134–35).
He does not take himself seriously as an artist, and this is amply illustrated at the comically anarchic management seminar at L'Esterel.
The trainees are middle-class conformists, businessmen who are as
predictable as their programs. Sam Tate, the organizer, trying to

break with tradition and treat the seminar as a new art form, arranges for Jake to talk to the group on "Artistic Imagination, Morals, and the Business Community." But things go awry. Jake speaks cynically about artists and critics, and tells the businessmen that they are very comfortably off compared to him because they follow a bureaucratic pattern and do not have to worry about their moral responsibility, since the company takes care of that, seeing to it that other customers and competitors get "screwed" (*GT,* 163–65). Pandemonium ensues. Arguments get rowdy and just stop short of violence. The comic anarchy, however, dramatizes the cost of Jake's naive honesty, and is simply one more instance when Jake Price has to pay a price for what he learns about power and relationships.

In his attempt to get at the truth of things, Jake suffers—sometimes trivially, but sometimes significantly. His liaison with Marie-Ange gets him a free studio atop a three-story loft. The studio and his first night's sex with Marie-Ange are parodied as a "ritual fruition" of art (*GT,* 30). Jake is able to live rent-free—something he has always wanted to do along with having to pay no income tax—but a sudden fire one night in an electroplating shop below destroys the studio, causes him to fall through a tarpaper roof, burn a leg, and crash amid a "flock" of garbage cans (*GT,* 115–24). He realizes with a jolt the heavy price to be paid for trying to break out of the social pattern, that is, for trying to live without a normal lease or without friends close by. Fortunately, he is not altogether cut off from the city pattern, for his friends come to his rescue once again, providing him with shelter and food.

Jake's most significant lessons are in sex and politics, and come from Marie-Ange and Roger Talbot respectively. Roger is first a shining star in the political firmament, but his luster dims and he is shown to be more of a scapegoat than a culture-hero. Yet his almost religious vision of Canada redeems many of his failings. For her part, Marie-Ange is a singular *lusus naturae* (in Roger's words) (*GT,* 42), but her sexual largesse and French Canadian charade are marks of desperation and fakery. In her prodigal sexuality, Marie-Ange is the opposite of Roger, whose quieter, more introspective nature makes him self-centered. Both become, then, illustrations to Jake of sex and politics as games of touch.

Marie-Ange plays the oldest game of touch as free sexual dalliance. Although she talks like a stilted academic, she has the soul and emotions of a promiscuous woman. Of English parentage and the former

Angela Robinson of Stoverville (who first appeared as "Bicultural Angela" in *Around the Mountain*), she has exchanged a narrow puritanical
upbringing for a French Canadian identity that thrives in the nation-
alist milieu of the University of Montreal. A CBC broadcaster and
film-maker, she has renounced her old ways of inhibition and has become hedonistic: "I'm not one of those bores who go on about their
state of grace, or worse, your state. I take the line that if you're
saved, you're saved, and if you're damned, you're damned, and either
way there's not much you can do about it, so you might as well enjoy
yourself" (*GT* 38). Marie-Ange's hedonism, however, has a desperate
ring to it as if it were reacting vehemently to a predetermined pattern. Caught in God's game of touch, she tries to reach His arms by
an all-too-human and liberal love. Her recurring dream of deliver-
ance, where she feels upborne in "sunlight, emptiness, and the arms
of God" (*GT*, 79), connects with her repeated patterns of free love,
where her prolific bedroom activities are an attempt to love her way
into understanding people. It is her political program, a way of finding a correspondence to the divine love she subconsciously seeks. Her
names (both in English and French) are apt significations of her spiritual yearnings, for she is a Mary revered by Roger and Jake, and she
is angelic (Ange; Angela) in her joy. Although her magnificat of sex
and her assertion that public virtue is dull and fragile (*GT*, 103)
mark her inclination to orgiastic self-release, Marie-Ange is not a
simple moral type. Her mythological emblem is Alcestis, as Roger
points out (*GT*, 101–2), and she is pursued by several lovers whom
she accommodates variously. In more familiar mythology, she is a
Canadian version of Eliza Doolittle because she is a Stoverville girl
transformed into a French Canadian CBC broadcaster with a
Québecois accent. Her most visible transformation is in the body-
painting scene, which develops out of the paint-in at Duncan's in
honor of Jake's narrow escape from death by fire. Her body becomes
a living canvas for Chris, Duncan, and Jake, but instead of looking
like a naked human, Marie-Ange looks strangely inhuman, "like a
statue of a goddess" (*GT*, 135). Yet this goddess is part of a decadent
cult of touch. She is treated as an object rather than a person, and
Jake feels guilty about having done "something mean" to her. When
at the end of this scene, Duncan breaks into a bitter protest-song
about a social calamity, this focuses the guilt.

There is little surprise when Jake feels he is better off with the
virginal Yvonne rather than with the promiscuous Marie-Ange.

Yvonne, after all, "doesn't promise you anything by hinting around, and then pulling back and claiming she didn't mean it. She makes it clear that a 'no' is a 'no' " (*GT*, 155). Yvonne is more honest than Marie-Ange. Unlike the latter, she retains her own identity. She accuses Marie-Ange of being something of a fake, of not really caring about Quebec or the French and of just using them as a means to her own egotistical self-gratification of the senses. The only thing that appears to touch Marie-Ange at the core is sex, and although she wins Duncan at the end, this gain is really a loss, for their perverse "swinging" (especially at the noisy, vulgar, mod discotheque Grandma's Antimacassar) cannot disguise their desperate attempt at self-liberation.

Sex, then, becomes a violent game in the body-painting scene and the final gathering of the Roger–Marie-Ange–Duncan trio at Grandma's Antimacassar. First, Marie-Ange's body is violated garishly by men who act as if in contempt of the flesh. Next, Marie-Ange becomes the reason for a decisive quarrel between Roger and Duncan.

But the commonplaces of men and women together in their games of sexual or romantic touch are not isolated in relief. They are allied to the more public business of politics, where the game is to try to keep in touch with society and the nation. Here, Roger Talbot becomes the principal dramatic figure, particularly because of his talent and conscience. A professor of economics at the University of Montreal who scorns artists as "political nullities" (*GT*, 19), Roger has "terrific energy" (*GT*, 22) and is considered by some to be one of the ten most important men in Canada (*GT*, 31). An expert in public financing of welfare and education programs, Roger is commissioned by the government to work on a complex federal-provincial health-services scheme. A staunch federalist, he is branded *un vendu* by Quebec nationalists, but this hostility is nothing new in his life. Under the autocratic rule of Duplessis, he had been an outlawed radical who refused to remain silent. He had stood sane and clear in the face of demagoguery (*GT*, 34) and now thinks of himself as an International Socialist. Yet he is keenly aware that "if you want to get reforms across, you go where the power is" (*GT*, 35). The problem for him is that he has little real political power, except that given to him by a ministerial function. He has no power base with the Quebec populace, and he knows that his ideal of a country of rational men is an exaggerated dream (*GT*, 35). Yet he does not abandon his vision of Canada as a potentially great country where justice can be had for all without war. This idea of public justice without violence appears in several of Hood's short stories and novels, and it gives *A Game of Touch* a philosophical undercurrent that travels deeply and widely. What might first appear to be a sociological laboratory experiment is really "a religious idea, finally, man acting out the instinct to justice, without war" (*GT*, 41). Roger's salvific scheme is a form of grace, a cure for many of the disturbed and disturbing consequences of sin.

Roger Talbot becomes a scapegoat, "one of those men," according to Marie-Ange, "who attract other people's burdens" (*GT*, 40). In the sometimes demonic environment of Ottawa, where it is "hellishly cold, and hideously ugly" (*GT*, 40), he is the singular harbinger of good news—a sort of evangelist who spreads the good news of Canadian identity. As he says to Marie-Ange:

You see, what we have in this chilly provincial spread of geography is a kind of sociological laboratory. We aren't revolutionaries and we aren't nihilists; we don't have any destructive myth about our manifest metaphysical destiny, like the Americans. We don't have the Negroes either. Our languages aren't really the barrier that the colour of your skin can be. . . . Once it's socially desirable to know both French and English, all over the country, when citizens of Ottawa or Vancouver learn that it's fashionable to open *Le Devoir* in a restaurant or the subway, we'll have reached the stage where the country can become what it may become—the only nation in the world to solve its internal problems and become politically mature without force. That may seem to you just an idea among a hundred others. I tell you, Marie-Ange, to me it's the most pressing idea there is. (*GT*, 40–41)

There is a strong element of fantasy in this vision because it is more a willed dream than a practical goal. But it is perhaps a necessary fantasy, for no nation can survive without vision. It marks Roger apart from other men because he participates in a myth. He sees himself in the role of Herakles, who goes around "doing good, righting wrongs, and bringing order into myth" (*GT*, 102), and he knows that power is the politician's fundamental motive. So fantasy and reality merge in his character, although the more involved he becomes in his project, the more distanced he grows from the populace. Roger is a clever theorist. He knows the sources of political power and the emblems of "great unconscious tides" of dissatisfaction. He reaches with his mind the "bottomless, humiliating wound in the unspoken darkest reaches" of Quebeckers' lives (*GT*, 89). Yet no amount of theory or rational thought can save him from the hostility of ultranationalists. His conscience is irrelevant to pragmatic politics, as he is bluntly reminded by the cynical minister who drops him after having exploited him as a "stalking-horse" and "straw man" (*GT,* 185). Roger cannot lie or say nothing under the guise of saying something important (*GT,* 182). He cannot stay with political patterns any more than he can stay with touch-football plays or paint-in patterns. In the very first game of touch, Roger is the only one unable to run the patterns (*GT,* 14). At Duncan's paint-in, Roger is the only one whose style does not fit with the styles of the others. He retreats to a corner and everything he paints looks "tight and curled up, unrelated to the rest of the wall." Roger never even steps back once to see what the others are doing (*GT,* 128–29). In politics, he cannot be retained by the government because he does not fit in with either the other politicians or Quebec nationalists. The justice-seeker becomes the unjustly maligned. As a public figure he is in "an exposed position" (*GT,* 110), scrutinized by his enemies and vulnerable to innuendo. Though a bilingual Canadian, he is considered by Quebec extremists as a "secret Englishman, a tool of Toronto capitalism" (*GT,* 111).

Roger Talbot is really the most interesting character in the novel and often threatens to displace our interest in Jake altogether. Some critics, deceived by the most superficial parallels, see him as a representation of Pierre Trudeau, but Roger's style and performance are quite different from Trudeau's. For one thing, he is at heart a man of simple affections whose life has grown so complicated that he misses his pastoral past (*GT,* 61). In spite of a reference to his "dark powerful face," which gives him the look of "a pirate or an Italian movie star" (*GT,* 22), Roger is never as glamorous as Trudeau was in his heyday, and he never has the wide base of popular support that Trudeau once possessed. Moreover, his "religious vision" of Canada is far more radical than any of Trudeau's plans which, for all their celebrated intellectual rigor and moral propriety, never accommodate themselves without prejudice to political and social reality. Besides, Roger's idea of justice for all, although reminiscent of Trudeau's appeal for a "just society," is really a biblical theme and damages his career because it is far ahead of his countrymen's preoccupation with materialistic and chauvinistic issues. Roger is the ineffectual intellectual, the mocked and resented outsider who is sacrificed to society's patterns. He is essentially good and honest, but he cannot play society's games by its rules. His gift of improvisation is a radical disadvantage to him in a society that insists on common participation by common consent and convention. But he is not a tragic figure because he does not recognize certain important patterns. He knows that when he leaves politics to return to academic life (another circular movement in the book), the political climate will be easier and his economic scheme might pass. His undying faith in federalism gives him the courage to endure middle age and loneliness, and this is not such a bad finish to his story, after all.

The ending pulls various patterns together and carries us into Jake's accommodation to reality. A bungling artist with an undeveloped identity, who entertains naive desires to live rent-free, tax-free, and unattached to any other individual, he learns how far he has swung away from innocence. In the final chapter, he climbs a hill and looks down from above to see several games of touch in a park. He sees "distinct groups of players intermingling, then separating out" (*GT,* 187), just like the characters in his story who never blur our image of him but keep themselves separate and clear. Jake, however, joins them in the city's pattern—with one significant difference. He is not fully communal for he does not like the idea of picking up strangers for an impromptu game of touch. This is an irony when we recall how quickly he was accepted by a group when he first arrived in the city.

In sum, although there are flaws in Hood's novel—undeveloped subsidiary characters who are used like stock types; highly academic chunks of dialogue for Roger and Marie-Ange—*A Game of Touch* is a successfully didactic work of realism. The urban environment is thoroughly credible; the emblematic epiphanies are effectively dramatic; and the didactic suasion gives the novel weight to compensate for its vehement social insularity. This is a searching investigation into the problems of finding a place in a troubled society. But it is, by and large, a calm investigation—richly funny at times, rigorously intellectual at others—without any seething anger or a visible metaphysical shudder.

Chapter Six
You Cant Get There From Here

In *You Cant Get There From Here*,[1] Hood surprises all those critics who charge that he fails to deal adequately with the problem of evil. Although richly comic in many ways, *You Cant Get There From Here* is an anatomy of human failure—a demonic satire on the corruptions of truth, justice, and love in the earthly city, St. Augustine's city of man, whose citizens are vessels of wrath, greed, and misery. Hood's texture is weightily credible in details of topography, economics, politics, and technology, and it vibrates with the excitement of a thriller, but its more substantial underpinnings are of a different nature. Concerned as it is with anatomizing man's corruption, it offers an allegorical vision of despair—a black world in total contrast to the predominantly white one of *White Figure, White Ground*.

Hood calls his book a Menippean satire, borrowing Northrop Frye's term for a form that sees evil and folly as "diseases of the intellect."[2] Presenting his characters as mouthpieces of ideas, Hood gives us "an intellectual anatomy" of "all the modes of existence and struggle in a new society."[3] That is why he has a cabinet of good and bad members, and chunks of maddened rhetoric where he parodies intellectual pretension and eccentricity. His book thrives on caricature and a free play of incident that builds up his observation of the structure of society. The flexibility of Menippean satire enables him to engage in conflicts of ideas in a form that freely combines fantasy and morality. The book has an exuberance of erudition and humor, and sometimes buries some of the characters under an avalanche of their own jargon. But the overwhelming pattern is that of a disintegrating society, and the tone is shaped by a conception of despair.

Normally we would be tempted to call this an ironic mode (and some critics have done just that), but Hood's irony does not follow Cicero's formula, Quintilian's description, or the earliest dictionary definitions. With him, it is not a device of saying one thing and meaning another, and when surprises occur in the plot, this is simply because truth is slow to reveal itself. Hood gives us epiphanies that frequently surprise us by their impact, and it is precisely this impact that makes him more than a merely cerebral artist.

There are many surprises in *You Cant Get There From Here,* and the satire on life's vanities is undeniably corrosive. Illusion is a theme and mood, and the novel's structure reflects this. As is characteristic of Hood's long fiction, there is a three-part structure, called intriguingly "On the Surface," "Underground," and "Underwater"—captions that portend a story of multi-level shifts, inconstancies, and mysteries. The African setting is a fictive model of sinister, treacherous changes. Deceit runs through everything. Characters are often not what they seem to be, and the plot plays a few tricks. Everything is contaminated or soiled—religion, art, politics, money, and love.

Hood builds up a credible locale that seems particularly African while it is also a fantasy or metaphor for the universal Shadow—the dark underside of our psyche that we often shrink from. His Africa is not the surrealistic continent of magic as in Audrey Thomas's *Blown Figures* or an exotic excuse for glamorous literary fantasy as in John Updike's *The Coup.* Leofrica is a misty, dusty vanity; its primitivity a nest for the darkness in man's heart, and its neocolonial follies a symptom of universal delirium. Leofrica, a name that suggests Leo the MGM lion, the lion in Blake and Dante, and the British imperial lion, is given a geography of dualities. The coastline, river, dry highlands, and fertile lowlands become an imaginative geography of human destiny, marking the soul's descent into Ulro or Hell. The basic dualism arises out of the tribal split between the highland Ugeti, a nomadic group analogous to the biblical nomads, and the agrarian Pineals, the more resourceful group that is feared by the Ugeti. The atmosphere is predominantly misty, and Newport, the capital of the country, is literally built on mud.

Newport is the earthly city ordained to disaster because its foundation is mud, the very spits and "constantly shifting bottom" of a river that is dangerously mutable. The shifting sands bring to mind Dante's Malbowges. Water, usually a dual symbol, is not here an emblem of regeneration or purification, but in its "boil and swirl" (*YC,* 100) is a sign of chaos and death. The river-bed is uncertain (*YC,* 55) and the water is "freighted with mud and sand and dung" (*YC,* 7). The outskirts of Newport suddenly become a treacherous swamp in which a Land Rover gets stuck (*YC,* 60). "Through this unsystematized *paysage* runs a network of constantly shifting paths, discernible only to the veteran eye, narrow, virtually hidden by overhanging grasses or by piles of muddy sand" (*YC*, 59). Aboleas, a marketing center, is equally deceptive in appearance. Fields that seem "solid, earthy, well planted," quake beneath motor transport and transform themselves into bogs under very moderate weight. Great holes in the ground suddenly appear in the middle of what is supposed to be a broad highway (*YC*, 74). This is like Blake's Ulro of rock, sand, and sterility. It is also like Dante's Hell. The country "fools you" (*YC*, 99), and the hot wind, as in Dante's infernal geography, compounds the mood of damnation (*YC*, 96).

The key word in this geography is "shifting," which applies equally to water, sand, rock (there is a fatal landslide), and politics. Mass opinion shifts in the plot, as do the fortunes of the main characters. Even the title of the book in Michael Macklem's original cover design suggests uncertainties. As Patricia Morley has pointed out, the "witty cover design and title page play upon the paradoxes in the title; you can, you can't, get there, get here, from here."[4]

The first section, after the mood-setting symbolic landscape, moves like a thriller and draws us into the hectic activity of Independence Day in the Republic. It is 8 A.M. on 1 May—May Day, Hood's clever signal of the stress and distress to come. The President/Prime Minister–designate, Anthony Jedeb, has to select his cabinet, upon the advice of Clive Maharaj, his confidential secretary. Jedeb is accompanied to the festivities by a young friend, Amélie de Caulaincourt, a sexy stranger to Ugeti and Pineal ways, who, like the conventional heroine of romance, has had her travails. The names of the characters indicate Hood's cosmopolitanism and craft. Anthony Jedeb is both Western and Eastern in nomenclature; Clive Maharaj suggests British Indian history; while Amélie brings to mind the French colonial fact. Hood's Leofrica is a fictional paradigm of universal colonialism, for it combines East and West (Asia, Africa, Europe, America), primitive and civilized, Christian and non-Christian. Some critics have concentrated on the deep divisions between Ugeti and Pineal tribes to draw parallels between Leofrica and Canada, but the tribal friction and international subterfuge serve a far wider purpose; they become an expression of Hood's interest in social neurosis, the irrational fear that one group of people can have of another. This is not a distinctively Canadian phenomenon, but a universal malaise.

The mixture of names and ethnology points to divided sensibilities. The Ugeti, "a lean and undersized folk" (*YC*, 11), have a cattle-cult and are paranoid about the Pineals, who are "an agreeable folk, unwarlike and slow to anger" (YC, 20). The Pineals have a clear-cut, promising economic future. Their agriculture thrives on the greater groundnut (here Hood offers a very impressive lesson in agriculture and economics), and they adapt readily to town life, even to city life (YC, 20). But Ugeti legend and myth teach that "the Pineals are eternally hostile and aggressive, always threatening to cross the South Ugeti and invade the highlands" (YC, 12). Jedeb tries to control this paranoia and foster social justice. His inaugural speech sets up Leofrica as "a haven to the wandering and the oppressed . . . a peaceable new nation" where "there will be no repression of opinion, no preferment of one economic goal before another, when both are equally pressing" (YC, 23). Even-handed justice is his ideal, and his cabinet appointments are made to pacify both tribes and achieve political efficiency. But tribal distrust runs deeply and pathologically, and it is only a matter of time before mass delusion breeds almost hallucinatory terror.

Jedeb, born an Ugeti, tries to be impartial as Prime Minister, but finds at the last that he is considered a traitor. Clive and Amélie are two spies whose selves are at war with politics. Held in high repute by many of his colleagues, Clive Maharaj is considered "immensely discreet . . . a man above subornation" (YC, 36), but these appear to be false impressions, for Clive is later destroyed by his own treachery. Amélie, for her part, is a clever spy who exploits Jedeb's sympathy, kindness, and love in order to deliver the country into Soviet hands. She tantalizes Jedeb by her beauty and then betrays him. She is a demonic Enitharmon, and serves to divide the plot into two cults of female will. Together with Galina Semyonovna, the Russian Ambassador's beautiful wife, she epitomizes feminine sexual allure, and, in contrast to Imine, the Ugeti Cow-woman, she is an earthly mistress at an opposite pole to the Mother Goddess.

Other divisions abound. The cabinet members soon bicker among themselves. Colonel Naumba, stentorian chief of the Leofrican constabulary, looks to the welfare of his own platoons. Lev-Paul Minho, a famous old-line Socialist, supports a double currency. Taylor Smithson, the bank manager who runs the Ministry of Finance, conserves capital for himself. The Minister of Justice, Abdel Entebbe, who specializes in divorce cases, turns out to be "a consummate rogue" (YC, 26). Jedeb is himself a divided man, split by his own confusions and inexperience—as his memorandum pad shows:

Encourage industry. Query: what industry?
Revive University College.
Or should primary schools come first? See Bill Menthe.
Power grid, how construct?
Also communications. NB: see about TV.
Census.
After census, free elections.
Underline *free,* yes, but how?
Name for the money?
What are pyrolusites, in technical terms?
Designs for stamps; must be local artist. Use my picture?
Postal services. My God!
How compute gross national product?
Press services. Query: suppress *The Times?*
No illiberal measures. (*YC,* 10)

This is wonderful satire. The country is a *tabula rasa* for the new regime, and it is like "living in a balloon filled with a very thin, rather intoxicating gas" (*YC,* 38).

Even the diplomatic corps are divided in their risible ways, and Hood satirizes them as they turn up for the Independence Day Ball in their respective vehicles: a specially imported Cadillac sedan with bullet-proof windows for the American Ambassador; a taxi for the Soviet Trade Commissioner; and shank's pony for the Albanian Minister (*YC,* 30). The Americans seek to control the economy, whereas the Russians show a great interest in engineering and geology. Each side has its own busy espionage service, and in spite of the ultimately sinister consequences, there is much anarchic comedy in their clashes. Some of the greatest comedy lies in the secret mission of the Russians, who, contrary to all expectations, do not really want Leofrica, but seek, instead, to throw it, chaos and all, to the bemused Americans.

Comedy vies with political seriousness in Part One. Jedeb's inauguration literally gets off to a rickety start, as the dais for the dignitaries begins to shake under the collective weight of the guests. Dr. Lentulus's solemn and tediously verbose opening address prolongs the comic agony, and leaves just enough time for Jedeb's speech to conclude before the platform collapses (*YC,* 24). The inaugural luncheon provides heavy fare, and Clive Maharaj pays the price of flatulence for drinking Pineal beer (*YC,* 35). Later, the ball at Government House is marked by heavy rain and damp skyrockets that fizzle, sputter, and go out inauspiciously (*YC*, 51).

Hood draws correspondences between politics and religion. Newport is meant to be a peaceful kingdom, haven for all who seek salvation from injustice and misery (*YC*, 23). The wandering Ugeti are like biblical nomads, and their stark land subjects them to blights of drought and famine that suggest the plagues on Egypt (*YC*, 11). Jedeb's history strengthens the scriptural analogies. His parents make a *hegira* in the wild (*YC*, 12), and Jedeb becomes a political patriarch with a cabinet of twelve, his chosen followers. He is a Christological figure, as Hood himself indicates, the first two letters of his name being "Je," and "Anthony" suggesting the first hermit, "the first Christian spiritual practitioner to go out into the desert."[5]

There are sacramental emblems. Ugeti *rites de passage*, where a herdsman's vest is given to an adolescent boy, are similar in concept to "the Christian notion of the armour of righteousness" (*YC*, 12). Interfoods, the American conglomerate, is a secular Eucharist, but the Americans, at least those like their Ambassador Ruggles, counsel the doctrine of the "invisible presence" in the country (*YC*, 38). The UN Articles of Charter serve as universal scripture (*YC*, 22), but the country, subject to native mythology, adopts animals as its religious emblems. The Ugeti have their totemic cult of the cow, replete with an oral epic narrative, "all derived from legends of the sacred bull-god, his various consorts, and the spirits who make the grass grow, weather spirits" (*YC*, 12–13). The Pineals, on the other hand, have serpent-worship as their central creed. Their theology is a weird blend of anthropology, sex, and religion, as Abo, their water-serpent, is believed to creep onshore and deflower virgins. The town of Aboleas gets its name from Abo, and "Aboleas" means roughly "Big fuck" in English (*YC*, 39). As Ambassador Ruggles explains: "Abo the water-serpent is a symbol of supernatural agency, an animistic version of the power of the river, but reversed, so that instead of going from the land to the ocean, he creeps back out of the ocean onto the shore. It's a heavily sexual image" (*YC*, 39). And it yields some outrageous satire, as when the Pineal women sneak into town at night, come down to the shore, and spend hours embracing the oil pipeline laid by the Americans. The line looks like a big snake to them, so, out of their combination of fear and love, the women straddle the pipeline, hug it, and croon: "They know there's oil in there and it becomes semen in their feverish imaginations. Sometimes they put holes in the outer wall of the pipe from sheer enthusiasm, but they aren't the ones who do deliberate damage. It's getting to be quite a ritual by now. After the women have had their go—and apparently some achieve orgasm—the men come" (*YC,* 40).

The natural religion is a deformed version of theology. The worship of Imine and Abo are part of what Frye calls the psychology of the Fall.[6] Imine's cult shows its devotees' helpless dependence on Mother Nature for all their ideas. Imine is the female will awaiting fulfillment by the visitation of the male deity. She is the waiting-womb and shows what Frye terms "a desire to prolong the helplessness of the perceiver and his dependence on the body of nature which surrounds him."[7] The Pineals' serpent-worship symbolizes "an earthbound, cold-blooded and often venomous form of life imprisoned in its own cycle of death and rebirth."[8] In Blake's *Book of Urizen* a brazen serpent hung by Moses on a pole symbolizes the death of African civilization, and *You Cant Get There From Here* draws its own pattern of doom for Leofrica.

In Part Two, the religious associations become infernal rather than beatific or salvific. The Russian engineers leave Newport for hill country, but without maps in largely unexplored terrain, they journey into a veritable hell of body and spirit. The mountains look like "real hell," an "honest-to-God hell" (*YC,* 54), and the Soviet convoy makes the sound of the Last Trump (*YC,* 60). It is like the Red Sea crossing as a Land Rover gets stuck in the mud (*YC,* 60), and instead of dispersing their culture in the Third World, the Soviets become a diaspora of victims. The heat builds, and famine and drought seize the land. Ralph MacSweyn, manager of the local branch of Interfoods, feels like Joseph in exile, and draws an analogy between Leofrica's "lean kine" and Egypt's (*YC,* 89). Though they believe themselves to be children of God (*YC,* 143), the Ugeti shrivel. Their small herds of runty cattle dwindle, and their spindly herdsmen stand forlornly (*YC,* 149).

In such a fated land, the Russians look to science for redemption, but they are destined to probe in mud. Newport, as in the Judeo-Christian myth of creation, shows that the city of man comes out of slime (*YC,* 63). The Russian expedition led by Professor Kuzmich encounters quicksand, boiling and swirling water, and later "total silence" (*YC,* 100–102). As the Russian scientists slog through the heat and mud, the diplomats weave their way dangerously through intrigue that gets hotter with the June weather. The paranoia in the diplomatic corps grows, and Amélie is used as a secret agent to destroy both Jedeb and the Americans.

The political conflicts are not without comedy. In one very brisk, very funny scene, Ted Dogwa, the Minister of Trade and Export, is overwhelmed by Lev-Paul Minho, the Minister of Labor and former friend of Trotsky. Minho is warm-hearted, learned, but nevertheless "partly lunatic" (*YC*, 63). All Dogwa wants to know is if the country can make bricks and sell them, but what he gets in response to his query is a wild rhapsody of economic theory that owes "much to Marx and perhaps more to Major Williams and his doctrine of Social Credit":

"Passing over the theoretical question of the definition of communality and ignoring the history of, say, the Proudhonian commune, the Leninist soviet, or the otiose meanderings of the Owenites," said Mr. Minho sturdily, even angrily, "we may allow ourselves to commence with social wealth. The mud belongs to no-one, or to all. Axiomatic, I believe. The exploiter who takes from me my right in the mud—if I possess such right— has sequestrated a portion of my social being. . . ."

Oh, Abo, Abo, Abo, mighty fucker, thought Mr. Dogwa, release me from my stupidity, help me to understand what he is saying. All I want to know is can we make bricks and sell them. (*YC*, 62–63)

Minho's inspired lunacy frustrates Dogwa, who turns quite mad himself. During his walks around town, Dogwa carries a small chisel and claw hammer, and when nobody is looking he knocks off bits of brick for samples (*YC*, 64). One night he suffers a rebuke when a householder empties a slop-pail over him (*YC*, 65).

The other tensions are not comic, as Dogwa himself perceives:

Mr. Uvalele, he heard, was under constant strain because of his responsibility for the Soviet mining engineers. Mr. Smithson was trying to finalize plans for the issue of the new money. Mr. Menthe, seen now and then entering or leaving his school building (built, Mr. Dogwa opined, of inferior brick) sometimes muttered bewildered sentences about the opinions of his students. Mr. Soyede was locked in a power struggle with Mr. Smithson over the question of the design of the first issue of banknotes. Mr. Entebbe and Colonel Naumba were likewise profoundly at odds over the status of the Constabulary and their right to lay charges and initiate prosecutions. Dr. Ibahi complained at all times of the shortage of nurses and medicines. Mr. bar-Iljian seemed to have sunk into bewildered nonentity. Only the

Prime Minister, the Minister without Portfolio, and Mr. Maharaj, seemed to retain the drive and buoyancy of pre-inaugural times, still scarcely eight weeks into the past. (*YC,* 65–66)

Some of the consequences of these tensions are deadly. Mr. Menthe, the Minister of Education, is forced to go into the streets to find teachers and beg for equipment (*YC,* 69). One hot June he suffers a fatal heart attack under the stress (*YC,* 73).

The old currency declines steadily in value, and a couple of tons of UN scrip, the paper money, vanish one night (*YC,* 78). The heat continues to build as intrigue comes to a boil. Clive Maharaj turns out to be a Judas, and Amélie, a fatal trap for the Prime Minister. Jedeb, dizzied by the speed of events, proves to be just what Amélie sums him up as: a kind, good man, but politically incapable. He becomes increasingly isolated from his cabinet and people. His reflectiveness locks him up in his own solitude. Without his old parents' shrewdness and toughness—tested in a crucible of persecution and flight—Jedeb finds all his hopes destroyed. The herbal soup he uses as a meal to promote brotherhood does not heal the rift between him and his society (*YC,* 142). The harsh world of reality breaks into his consciousness, and Jedeb, accused of having betrayed Pineal interests, recognizes the murderousness of words such as: "nation, faction, culture, tribe, people, race, clan, proletariat, class" (*YC,* 142).

Leofrica becomes desolate with its restless insecurity and violence—the type of neocolonial chaos that writers such as V. S. Naipaul and N'gugi wa Thiongo write so powerfully about in their novels. However, all the political flux and instability are not uniquely African. They are universal disorders that man has brought upon himself everywhere in the world, because he has not been able to exercise justice in his relationships with other men.

Everything in Leofrica is soiled. Newport, we have already seen, is built on mud which the Russian scientists are doomed to explore in vain. Interfoods is run by Ralph MacSweyn, whose surname is an apt phonetic pun because there is something peculiarly swinish about his doctrine of imperial consumerism (*YC,* 31). MacSweyn caters to human lust for consumption, and lust, which originally meant "pleasure," is perverted into a monstrous appetite for self-indulgence. The point is developed by several examples. Ted Dogwa lusts after Galina Semyovna, just as MacSweyn, caricatured as a rapist with a "sexual member of disproportionate size" (*YC,* 83), lusts after Amélie. Erotic passion, certainly no taint in itself (as shown in the heaving, blissful copulations of Galina and her husband), is soiled by the personalities of Dogwa and MacSweyn.

Religion, sex, and money are linked to excrement or urine. The Dance of Imine is the dance of copulation where the cow-woman smears herself with cattle dung and retreats alone to a hillside to await impregnation by the god's lightning and rain (*YC*, 47). Amélie, who at one point conceals a microfilm in her anus (*YC*, 131), moves through an excremental phase, a mimesis of Imine's dung-smearing, when she buries herself in a pile of rotting cow-dung for a day in order to convince herdsmen that she is the daughter of Imine (*YC*, 136).

Hood's excremental and urinary vision, different from Swift's because it does not posit any *essential* debasement in human nature, creates explicit emblems. Ugeti sand-sculpture is an example of debasement in art because it is a parody of what psychologists call anal character. All babies play with their urine and feces before they are conditioned to regard this play as dirty, and this innocence is parodied by Hood when he describes Ugeti sand-relief: "The sculptor deposits a thick bed of sand in a tray or frame, dampens it thoroughly with his urine, then molds the relief with his hands. The finished panel, extremely abstract and formal, is then left to bake in the sun for a full season; it will then hold its form if handled with care. The slightest bump will cause the sand to fall from the frame, destroying the work completely" (*YC*, 113). All is mocking vanity, indeed, when such work is prized for its "poignant combination of fragility with stern harsh beauty of line" (*YC*, 113).

The excremental vision is also linked to money, which is one of the main characters in the book and which is treated allegorically in the manner of Spenser's Cave of Mammon. In Hood's novel, money and dung are interchangeable. Hood seems to remember Freud's point about the anal subject's pleasure in looking at his own feces.[9] Freud believed that the "unconscious identifying of faeces, gifts, and money influences many later social relations involving money."[10] In Hood's book, money is identified with excrement just as precious metals are in Thomas More's *Utopia*, where gold and silver are used for making chamber-pots and stools.[11] A sturdy Pineal longshoreman who needs to defecate uses a fistful of ten-dollar bills for toilet paper. He then allows the bills to float away over the water into "the ambiguous estuary" (*YC*, 178). Here money is certainly feces.

The contaminants in Part Two extend to the religious parody, though here the point is not excremental or urinary. The God-Bull is a parody of the Parousia (*YC*, 110), Imine's Tent is a version of the Tabernacle (*YC*, 112), and Amélie, a "goddam girl" who is "infernally pretty," works a demonic transubstantiation when she swallows high-risk microfilm (*YC*, 93–94). When the Albanian Minister Zogliu (whose surname shows how the characters run from A to Z— Anthony to Zogliu) offers Lance-Major Abdelazar a kingdom in exchange for the betrayal of Leofrica, the scene occurs in a helicopter and parodies Satan's mountain-top temptation of Christ (*YC*, 149).

Sometimes Hood's allegory is far-fetched, as when it turns the United States nuclear submarine *Aphrodite* into an illusion of Leviathan (*YC*, 90) and then into the "original love goddess" (*YC*, 153). But, in general, it helps carry the novel to apocalyptic climaxes.

Part Two builds relentlessly in excitement as the country tears apart and pulls Jedeb down with it. The Russians get lost in hellish country and suffer through a landslide of falling rocks (*YC*, 128). The country's double currency falls apart. Colonel Naumba cannot get military aid from either the Russians or Americans and feels totally betrayed. Clive's espionage is discovered. The *Aphrodite* runs aground in thick fog. Soyede is assassinated by Zogliu and Abdelazar, and the land suffers a blight that shrivels all life. Perhaps the most significant dramatic event, however, in terms of allegorical meaning is the spectacular oil fire which results when the American refinery ("pharaoh's palace" to MacSweyn—*YC*, 89) is sabotaged (*YC*, 125). The infernal radiance indicates how fire will combine with water as the two definitive symbols of apocalypse.

In Part Three, we see clearly that this is the only novel in which Hood permits no release from evil. Doom congeals around the heart of the comedy. Hood mocks political simpletons and their bloated rhetoric of false promises and impossible idealism (the pompous RIRU declaration of independence is a gem of parody (*YC*, 159) and even Jedeb is satirized.

An atmosphere of horrible atrocity develops. Clive Maharaj is blown up by a remote-control bomb that makes "the sound of the apocalypse" (*YC*, 179). His body is "simply atomized," and the image of Armageddon intensifies when a frenzied mob tramples Colonel Naumba to death (*YC*, 192). Torture becomes fashionable, and the civil war causes a new Ugeti *hegira* (*YC*, 188). The mass exodus leads to a river-crossing that suggests the Israelites' crossing of the Jordan into the Promised Land. The column of refugees chant the ancient Ugeti song of God the Bull, who welcomes them from exile. A rain-

storm and later a fire end the exodus (*YC,* 190–91), but not before
Jedeb's old parents are massacred.

Jedeb realizes too late that "some political situations are not via-
ble" (*YC,* 201), but his failing is not political ignorance as much as
it is moral innocence that cannot cope with reality. As a Christ figure, he suffers a stigmata when a long spike of wood drives itself into
his left heel (*YC,* 200), and he becomes an Everyman ("Antonio. An-
toine. Antony. Tony."—*YC,* 201). But this Everyman must die because "nothing goes right in Leofrica" and because he cannot turn the
country into a peaceable kingdom. His death occurs in darkness,
where he suffers under the signs of fire and water. His former love,
Amélie, had had her own trial by water when she once made a dangerous river-crossing at night (*YC,* 133), but Jedeb's water trial is an
infernal inverted baptism where, instead of being reborn by water and
the spirit, he is forced to drown himself to escape the rocks and bul-
lets of his pursuers. He remembers he had come naked into the world
(*YC,* 200), but he never has the chance to put on new garments of a
re-created being. This Christ figure descends into a hell, never to rise
again from the dead. And his tragic gloom is compounded by the fate
of the whole country. The pursuing mob are idiots who lose their
lives in the treacherous mudbanks as they chase Jedeb. The doomed
Jedeb cannot get anywhere from here. His clarity of mind cannot ex-
tricate him from a vortex of violence. Trapped in the earthly city
whose citizens are "vessels of wrath," he cannot reach the heavenly
city where "vessels of mercy" can console him. But his hunters are
also without consolation as they are left in the dark, firing at the hero
swallowed by water and mud.

You Cant Get There From Here is an impressive achievement. Hood
has never been anywhere near Africa, and what he knows about the
continent comes out of his reading. (He researched the groundnut,
for example, in an encyclopedia.) Yet his book is composed with loving attention to particularities of place. It has clarity and suppleness,
and never makes John Updike's error of relying on gorgeous Western
language in *The Coup* to dress up an eccentric view of African life.
Indeed, in a vital sense, it is not as much about Africa as it is about
fallen man. Jedeb's cabinet is not identified solely with Leofrica, but
becomes a multi-modal account of how we all live in the world. The
cabinet and Leofrica are destroyed by human folly, and though Jedeb
has a vision of justice for the common good, it is an unclear vision.
Without true vision, any country perishes.

Chapter Seven
The New Age / Le Nouveau Siècle

Encyclopedic Dimensions

Hood has described *The New Age* series as a long serial philosophical novel that uses all the materials of his life,[1] and taking a Coleridgean model, he makes a very wide range of miscellaneous references in a huge synthetic span in order gradually to allow connections to emerge.[2] In this as yet incompleted twelve-part *roman fleuve*, Hood is attempting to do "as fully, and as powerfully, and as many-modally, and as exhaustively" as he can what he is capable of achieving in long narrative.[3] The series begins in Toronto in the 1930s, then backtracks, but intends to catch up with the present decade, before culminating in the millennium. It brings together various periods of time in a single, wide focus, and without attempting to be a pyschological epic (like Proust's *Remembrance of Things Past*) it presents "spots of time," long passages of discursive rumination and moments of the self, as it confronts inherited or fresh experiences. The New Age is to be a massive story of Canada's "ranges of behaviour" or "moral possibilities"[4] reflected in the growth and development of Matt Goderich, Hood's occasionally pompous and naive protagonist, who is fundamentally good-natured and intellectually curious.

The bilingual title of Hood's epical *roman fleuve* confirms his intention, articulated in 1964, to unite in his writing the totality of Canadian culture ("la culture la plus intéressante du monde").[5] Whether, in fact, he will be able to realize such a massive ambition remains to be seen, but with a quarter of the series already published, we can appreciate the encyclopedic dimensions of the work.

We are as likely to find essays on axiology, socialism, and art as we are prone to find discussions of baseball, Dinky Toys, penny candy, and movies. Hood waxes as eloquently on James T. Farrell, Stephen Leacock, and Loyalist architecture as he does on Toronto's topography, railway routes, and the Eaton's catalog. His characters include figures from mythology and Catholic hagiography, eminences from the twentieth century, and ordinary people whose ordinariness is often placid without necessarily being dull. Although the first three novels are set in Ontario (particularly in Toronto and Stoverville) the New Age series is like a repository of Canadian history. Its themes dip into the past, sweep up some of the present, and plunge forward into the future with synoptic assurance and intelligibility, and reading them is a little like traveling down a long, glittering canal, as smooth as glass, whose cool transparency allows us to find the fascinating, shifting bed of our present age.

The New Age series looks everywhere for value—at religion, art, politics, history, economics, botany, architecture, literature, philosophy, technology, geography, sociology. It flows out of the documentary tradition of fiction—the kind specialized in by Dos Passos, Dreiser, and O'Hara—but widens into a secular analogy of Scripture, and this makes it an interestingly different species from anything else we have been accustomed to in our day.

Like James Joyce, Hood loves catalogs, etymologies, mythologies, and epiphanies. From Marcel Proust he obtains an inspiration to make an "intellectual analysis of the nature of historical time, the place of historical time in valuation."[6] He refuses to engage in Proustian analysis of psychology because twentieth-century psychology seems "so largely mere phrenology" to him, or else "a series of stand-up comedians recognition jokes."[7] Hood is always a witty writer and often parodic, but his style is not derivative. Like Anthony Powell, he is interested in the crisscrossing of people's paths and in the sense of an enormous society, but his wit attempts to deal with the totality of things. Although his long fiction is sometimes an alternating flux and outburst of citations, his apparently discrete way of expressing themes creates what Roland Barthes called "the allure of the connotation" where the end or final vision is always clarified by the writer's gestures and jests.[8]

What makes *The New Age* unique in Canadian literature is its method of cross-referencing within the domain of fiction. Hood's earlier novels (particularly *The Camera Always Lies* with its Proustian and classical allusions, and *You Cant Get There From Here* with its Christological emblems) had manifested an interest in vocabularies and their stylistics, but there the range was relatively narrow, and Hood used a simple linear or retrospective narrative. In *The New Age*, the narrator moves within a huge time span, and lines of character are continually crossing, as Hood indulges in free meditation on certain images.

The temporal arrangement allows for various points of view and fluctuating associations in the consciousness of the core protagonist, Matt Goderich, whose identity seems inextricably linked to that of his society. As Matt recounts the story of his own life and age—though not always in chronological sequence—Hood provides a large temporal perspective by pulling in the era of Matt's parents and by correlating (as Henry Fielding and Laurence Sterne did so cleverly in the eighteenth century, and as E. L. Doctorow does so naively in *Ragtime*) his fictional actions with an external time-scheme. The Goderich chronology relates to the dates of events such as the Winnipeg General Strike of 1919, the shrinking of the railroad in Eastern Ontario, the provocative Zionist issue of the 1920s, the Great Crash of 1929, the emergence of Jacques Maritain as a renowned philosopher, and the outbreak of the First World War. Matt undergoes an "intelligible evolution"[9] whereby he signifies himself as a person with a destiny, an object with a meaning in time. In the series, memory, "the mother of the Muses" (*GB*, 111), reconciles past with present in the "cunning corridors" of history where the divine mysteriously leaves footprints in the dust.

The Swing in the Garden

On the face of it, *The Swing in the Garden*,[10] the first part of the series, appears to mix documentary fact with fiction without telling a story in the conventional sense. The narrator is Matthew Goderich, in his mid-forties, who carries us back to his Toronto childhood in the 1930s. Although the characters are intensely alive, the realistic density appears to stifle an inherent *mythos,* and the chief problem— apart from Hood's Catholic optimism wherein virtue is made far more intellectually engaging than vice—becomes a question of form. An initial reading tends to make us feel with John Mills that the work is "undramatic and shapeless" and that though it is certainly a work of extraordinary richness, "it is not quite art."[11]

Hood does not resolve this problem by calling the work "the historical novel of social mythology and group awareness."[12] After all, *War and Peace* and *Remembrance of Things Past* are historical novels that are steeped in philosophies of time as they create their respective mythologies of groups and individuals, but they have shape, whereas

Hood's book at first appears to offer textbook subjects, thinly veiled by the mere suggestion of story. And the documentary cachet is certainly sealed by Hood's phrase for the book as "documentary fantasy."[13]

Hood's New Age series is millennial in that it will be completed in 1999 with a final volume intended to be a Canticle of Canticles. Hood suggests that the series should be read like the Bible, Blake's *Four Zoas,* or Joyce's *Finnegans Wake.*[14] This suggestion helps us to treat the book not so much as a conventional novel but as a piece of fiction that assimilates realism, satire, and romance. The overall shape is determined implicitly by what John Mills calls "a sequence of emblems, *topoi* for meditation,"[15] and far from being undramatic, *The Swing in the Garden* is very much a drama of awareness, in which Matt performs "an essentially religious, imaginative act," according to Robert Lecker, "by bringing together 'the spiritual intelligence and the world of the senses and the world of the incarnate.' "[16]

Although Hood imitates Proust (especially in the setting, which bears some resemblance to Combray in *Swann's Way,* and in excursions "into the country" and "down to the docks" which recast the ways of Guermantes and Swann), *The Swing in the Garden* has the archetypal form of a quest. Matt Goderich seeks his own paradise of unity with fellow men in a world redeemed by love and justice. Although the book ends with signs of war and death, it is largely a green world in contrast to the romantic white one of *White Figure, White Ground* or the black world of *You Cant Get There From Here.* The green is a liturgical symbol of hope, but it is also, fundamentally, a color of pastoral nature, and though Hood's vantage point is an urban world, his vision is pastoral—or perhaps what Polonius might have found "historical pastoral"—and moves through realism, romance, and satire.

By setting his story in Toronto and by projecting his direct vision of life through Matt, who is all his different ages at once, Hood is able to exploit the tensions of pastoral through the fresh sincerity of a swain. Behind this, of course, lies the idea of innocence, where pastoral tends to merge with the myth of the golden age, an Arcadia or Eden of the mind where life enjoys a pristine purity. The swain, still untainted by major evils, is an ideal innocent whose growing perceptions and conceptions join the simplified to the complicated, and Hood is able to keep contrasting ways of life in equilibrium. Matt is a normal bewildered man, looking back upon his childhood and adolescence and remembering the romance of youth through characters with romantic names such as Alanna, Laetitia, Alysoun, Elaine, Amanda, Isabelle, and Roland. Hood's pastoral is highly sophisticated—an urban product, and so, consistent with a primary condition of pastoral[17]—and its nostalgia, far from being primitive, is a Proustian yearning of memory that has an emotional function in the book.

Matt is like his biblical namesake, a synoptic evangelist whose voracious intellect internalizes a period's manners. By observing himself and others as if they were all in some film brilliantly directed by himself, "objectified on the big screen of our imagination" (*SG*, 133), Matt expresses changing social and cultural styles.

There is little humility in Matt, and certainly none of the sort traditionally associated with pastoral. His synchronous consciousness— the bringing into one picture different parts of a story—has no time for conventional humility, and it is only his sense of social inferiority that crystallizes the delicacy of feeling inherent in the social aspect of pastoral. What Matt is after is a general meaning for our age, and his reflections (sometimes as extended essays) lead us to judge the period "on the grounds of its enjoyment of, its special possession" of forms of communion among different generations. Robert Lecker, in a brilliant article, has already explored four forms of communion in the novel,[18] so there is no reason to rehearse them here, except to say that, with Matt's heightened awareness through aesthetic, communal, communicative, and spiritual experiences, the force of time is ever-present, "a constantly growing reminder that man is bound to finitude and the Fall."[19]

Original Sin is a felt doctrine in the novel. The very title indicates a swing away from the paradise of childhood, as it were. The pendular motion of the swing reminds us that "we will be reading about a journey between opposing states of time" for it joins two poles together—the garden's natural beauty and the garage's fallen state.[20] There is a young Adam (Sinclair—free of sin) in childhood's garden, and he is already envisaged as a scapegoat. This Adam never has luck on his side and is comically de-panted in the dark for being a notorious sissy (*SG*, 57–59). There is a watchtower at a crossing, and its symbolism is a reminder of God's surveillance of man. But the pattern of a divinely human comedy is set by several images in the first chapter. The landscape beyond the Goderich garden is dominated by the Hill, which is viewed as a "promised land" (*SG*, 6), and near it is the Bridle Path or the Bridal Path, associated not so much with

horses as with the "wedding march" or marriage—the fundamental
end of old comedy.

Matt's expulsion from his infant's Eden is marked by a movement
farther east—the symbolic direction of new mystery, knowledge, revelation, and life (*SG,* 32). After Eden, Matt nearly inherits death in
a vacant lot where he almost drowns in a dark water-filled hole (*SG,*
39). He later suffers a scar when he slips on a roller-skate during his
younger brother's christening, and this mark of pain and disgrace is
sometimes referred to by his mother, "not wholly jokingly," as "the
brand of Cain" (*SG,* 47).

In Chapter 2, Matt's swing from innocence dips deeper into the
darkness and frustration of the human heart. The cinema is a false
paradise that lives by its one-cent candy, Flash Gordon serials, news-
reels, cartoons, and trailers. The excruciating din outside sounds like
Gehenna or Armageddon, "or the awakening of the Divine Beast in
the Revelation to St. John on Patmos" (*SG,* 56). Adam Sinclair becomes the victim of the mocking prank whereby he is cruelly de-
panted.

Matt later acquires another scar. In what cannot be evaded as an
aural pun, he is *scathed* by his unrequited love for Beatrice Skaithe,
the *princesse lointaine* of the romantic satire in the plot. Beatrice remains the unattainable feminine ideal (like Dante's "blessed one")—
an image of perfection, but a Protestant one and incompatible with
Goderich Catholicism.

Because Hood's work is realistic in its portrayal of social life, when
Matt takes us back to childhood, he also takes us back to concepts
and feelings about such things as sex. Here the pastoralism is a dualistic attitude to sex in childhood and, as such, crystallizes Laurence
Lerner's identification of the paradox of childhood sexuality with the
paradox of Arcadia: "Sexless or free of sexual restraints: are not these
our two views of infancy? Childhood is the time when we have not
yet been troubled by sex; but it is also the time when (like the
nymphs in Tasso's chorus) we didn't have to wear clothes, and didn't
have a super-ego."[21]

Matt is sexually innocent until Georgie-Balls Bannon tells him the
first sex joke he can remember (*SG,* 33). The whole Bannon household seems soaked in sex. Esther Bannon (who plays a radical role in
Matt's sexual awareness) suggests her sensual biblical namesake as she
compels Matt to feel "the closed unapproachable untranslateable
structure of female experience, which no amount of feminist rhetoric,

designed to obscure the difference, can in fact deny" (*SG*, 33). But it is Letty Millen ("Letty" is a variant of "Laetitia" or "joy") at the top of Glen Road who earns six-year-old Matt's first romantic crush. He has "intensely lived fantasies" about her (*SG*, 34), and his confession of yearning marks a shift onto the child of the tradition of pastoral. Matt is no little rogue, but he is no angel either. We need only recall his cruel fun during the de-panting of Adam Sinclair to realize that this Arcadia is not as chaste as we might initially expect. Adam's seminudity evokes feelings of mockery or self-consciousness in Matt, who is not the pert child or underdog that Lewis Carroll's Alice is. Although the viewpoint at this stage of the text is a forty-year-old man's, we are nevertheless able to see the child-swain with misgivings about romance and sex.

Although the bulwarks of public morals (such as the nuns at school) assert their sway, in alliance with the Catholic Legion of Decency, Matt and his peers remain fascinated with revelations of Hollywood orgies and sex scandals (*SG*, 49). It takes a public chastisement by Marianne Keogh to humanize and civilize him about sexuality (*SG*, 146–49). A second lesson is had by the experience of androgyny, first as a playful curiosity about transvestitism (*SG*, 149) and then as an awareness of the Tiresian myth (*SG*, 193). Danger creeps into the subject with intimations of Adam Sinclair's homosexuality (*SG*, 193). Matt, a friend of Adam, is afraid of guilt by association. Now sexuality reaches a diabolic level where the erotic divides itself into the accepted and the taboo, and where doubt swirls about the paradise open to the child. Matt feels the force of social codes and cannot reconcile himself fully with nature and gain power over it. Clearly, this is no *Alice in Wonderland* dream-world where the fantasy mood is protected from reality.

In the final three chapters, Matt's special penchant for cross-referencing (*SG*, 116) is a symptom of his secular evangelism in that, by documenting the development of group manners and awareness in his society, he is a witness, like St. Matthew, to the unfolding of a special destiny. Matthew supplements the Gospel and his family name puts us in mind of the kingdom of God *(Godes rice)* that can be inherited by such grace. His moral imagination is helped by his parents: his mother, Isabelle, "the most sweetly reasonable person" he has known (*SG*, 64), makes a dogma of the open mind, fairness, and justice; while his father, Andrew, a Socialist philosopher who takes politics more seriously than his compatriots with a colonial mentality, endows Matt with a habit of mind to see conflict between dialectical poles resolved (*SG*, 68).

The Goderich house becomes a meeting-place for informal social gatherings (which even Jacques Maritain attends while in Toronto), and Hood builds up a cool, poised indictment of the "creeping fascism" in Canadian society of the time (*SG*, 73). The politics here are subtly pertinent to pastoral literature for, as William Empson points out, even proletarian art is usually covert pastoral.[22] Andrew Goderich, while no manual laborer, is sympathetic to the proletariat, becoming a sophisticated polemical voice for their social protests, and his university role strengthens the pastoral connection, for the university is the status symbol of twentieth-century North American culture, a replacement for the royal court of archaic pastoral. Andrew, however, is a critic of the university and a judge of his society, which considers him *persona non grata*.

Just as young Adam Sinclair feels cut off from his peers so also does Andrew Goderich feel isolated from the Canadians of his time. His special knowledge of axiology and international politics isolates him as a critic of moral style, but he is inexorably hemmed in by the form and pressure of class and money that constrain all Canadians of the period: Lawren Harris, for instance, who painted in a mode patronized by philistines; George Bannon "whose career was wholly out of his control"; even Bea Skaithe, who might otherwise have cared for Matt (*SG*, 84).

In spite of the strong criticism of the privileged classes, Matt does not identify with the proletariat or bourgeoisie. So, unlike his father, who "gave up a safe niche in the educational *apparat* to become a server of food," he cannot be classed with any group (*SG*, 197). As an art historian, he is a connoisseur of shapes and facts quite outside his father's sphere. He is not a representative of any single class, yet he is part of the pastoralism because he attempts to articulate conflicts between parts of his society, and by participating in art, which "makes us conscious of our links with other men throughout time, as well as allowing us to converse with the social world around us,"[23] Matt is able to tie "the interior worlds of multitudes together" (*SG*, 100).

The final three chapters gain momentum. Wheels dominate the children's games—Goderich is a name for an Ontario town whose name signifies a wheel—and the book has upward and downward movements. The Goderich family fortunes rise and fall; the country falls in to political and socioeconomic chaos; Matt's pride is lowered; and the "long fall" anticipated at the end is a season of human beastliness as World War II erupts.

A paradigm for such changing fortunes is obtained at the beginning of Chapter 4, where a reference to Sharon Temple, a Wilsonite structure, is misunderstood as a reference to Shirley Temple. In one fell swoop, the sacred becomes the profane. This is the chapter in which the Goderich restaurant business fails because of poor weather that puts off prospective customers (*SG*, 168). Matt learns of punishment and masculinist folly at the hands of Marianne Keogh, who spanks him for his public misbehavior (*SG*, 148). This is also the chapter where Andrew Goderich's fascination with the theology of the Fall is ironically justified by a superhuman will to malevolence. Matt sees in Art Comstock (a failed Arthur) "the first really disappointed and destroyed man" he's ever encountered (*SG*, 151), and Uncle Philip's collection of the *Boy's Own Annual* gives Matt his first glimpse of the symbols of war (tanks, trenches, planes) after he has missed earlier the omen in Monty McNally's toy Spitfire (*SG*, 130).

The book becomes decidedly demonic as Matt's magazines show him pictures of the destructiveness of war: "The terror, horror, murder, hate, fear, spill of intestine on rusted wire, separation of parts of bodies by screaming metal shards all were lodged there" (*SG*, 165). From the womb Matt has moved close to the tomb of history, and anticipates a cataclysm.

The biblical symbol for the end of the world is fire, and the final two chapters of *The Swing in the Garden* are dominated by destructive "fires." The only positive "fire" is associated with the Goderiches in that their fortunes, though burned up in Jackson's Point, will rise again like "the fabulous phoenix" (*SG*, 190). However, the downward spiral of "fiery" events continues elsewhere: a fire destroys the Lakeview (*SG*, 169); the Spitfires perform their deadly missions; Mr. Cawkell dies after stepping on a land mine; Mr. Weisman dies at Dieppe, "cut almost in half by machine-gun fire"; Mostyn McNally burns to death in a plane over the Ruhr, "riding the flaming fuselage all the way down" (*SG*, 210). Events do, indeed, make (in Matt's final words) "for a long fall" (*SG*, 210). The pastoral idyll ends, after its satiric and romantic phases, in deadly realism.

The ending makes us aware that Hood is preoccupied with the strengths and weaknesses of being human in Canada in the 1930s. There is an intrinsic parallel between Matt as infant and Canadian

society in its infantile, withdrawn state. Near the end of 1939, after
World War II has begun and Mostyn McNally has died, this society
has been forced to grow up, look outwards, become aware of social
and political conflicts in China, Spain, Germany, and even in itself.

The book, then, does, indeed, contain a story, and the superficial
placidity of the work submerges but does not truly obscure the
drama. For Hood, virtue is no less dramatic than vice, and in this
regard he is in the company of Greene, Mauriac, and Callaghan. His
characters bend all their strength, "not to deny the reality of sin,
but to show how it runs away to waste and nothingness in the ocean
of pure being."[24]

The Swing in the Garden is a quieter book than almost any of Hood's
earlier novels. Its pastoralism, however, is subtly complex for it is
structured so that the five chapters (equivalent to five acts of a
drama), "of about equal length, cover shorter and shorter periods of
time and seem more hurried and more eventful as they go on."[25] The
first human we see talking to baby Matt is the first to fall to enemy
fire. The "long fall" at the end suggests the widening arcs of evil, so
that a new age is "always before us, and always beginning," as Hood
says, and life is seen as "a conspectus of possible great events that
seem to widen out to infinity."[26] This attitude graces the theme of
innocence, for, like the dominant Adamic image in American literature of a hundred years ago, the most fruitful idea is that of an authentic wise innocent. However, Hood is not as vulnerable to moral
delusion as the nineteenth-century American writers were—
De Crèvecoeur, Emerson, Thoreau, Hawthorne—for he creates an air
of adventurousness and potential without asserting any dogma. Matt's
innocence is not that of prelapsarian Adam, whose moral position was
"prior to experience."[27] However, like the biblical and American Ad-
ams, he finds the world and its history open before him once he is
expelled from the Edenic womb of his infant environment. Where the
biblical Adam was a creator in his inventory of the world, Matt is
also a creator in his cross-references, ramifications, and annotations.

Hood's pastoral innocence is quite without the cheerless theology
of nineteenth-century American literature, where the "new man" or
innocent Adam dissociates himself from the past. Though Matt
quickly comes to realize the qualities of the fallen world about him,
he is not like Emerson's Adam, split between the past and the future.
The past is not an irremediable burden to him, and he does not seek
to escape it or burn it away according to Thoreau's injunction,[28] but

to understand and use it as a guide to the present and future. Unlike the American Adam of Holmes, who was "miraculously free of family and race, untouched by those dismal conditions which prior tragedies and entanglements monotonously prepared for the newborn European,"[29] Hood's innocent has a past and present peopled by many tribes—English, Scots, French Canadians, Protestants, Catholics, entrepreneurs, merchants, teachers, et cetera—all of whom are intensely human.

The stance in his pastoral is Canadian in its blameworthy, After-the-Fall style that does not, however, shrink from new tensions that provoke our conventional understanding of relationships between the new and the old, the individual and society, man and God, knowledge and innocence. In constructing Matt's relationship with the world, Hood digs into the Canadian landscape and finds referents for spiritual meaning in the physical scene, an outline of the ideal in the actual. The very forces that are often considered inimical to man—nature, technology, abstract reasoning, religion, et cetera—are placed in a total framework that sees life whole. Hood's pastoralism begins with an innocence that does not go unchallenged or untransformed. It is tested by drama (even if, at times, only intellectual drama) and strong intellectual illuminations charge it so that we grasp its special complexities, buoyant assurances, and troubling doubts about Canadian society growing up with Matt Goderich.

A New Athens

A New Athens[30] is Hood's Book of Revelation. Matt here is a pilgrim who begins with an excursion across a "twinned Ontario trail" and, as his mind composes relationships among a multiplicity of experiences, connects the human and divine through apocalyptic emblems that have an aesthetic intelligibility. Art historian that he is, with a degree in Art'n'Ark (Art and Architecture) from the University of Toronto, Matt uses the "Janus-headed impulse of the historian" ("the looking before and after") (*NA*, 58–59) to lead us from the new Athens, and Ontarian town, to a new Jerusalem, without diminishing the physical and visible worlds that art lives on.

Hood's craft reaches the apex of doubled realities. The anagogic method, used so strongly in *White Figure, White Ground,* now acquires a polished sophistication that combines the secular and sacral without the slightest bit of damage to the narrative. Beginning with the observable world, Hood undulates into the divine so that the power of his documentary fantasy transforms facts—what Wittgenstein calls "the totality of what is the case"[31]—into apocalyptic vision.

The four parts of the novel, as John Mills has observed, suggest the four elements.[32] Matt digs into the geography and archaeological lore of his place, even goes underwater in one sense, and then, after experiencing a pentecostal spirit of fiery faith, ascends through Mrs. Codrington's visionary art to the New Jerusalem that is an allegory of new Athens, the small town. The first section, which opens in June 1966, has Matt on a walking tour in the region between Brockville and Stoverville. Hood, who used biking and walking as pacesetters in *Around the Mountain,* develops an excursionary mood reminiscent of Wordsworth and Proust, both of whom wrote major works built around the image of walking trips. A Coleridgean element develops in Matt's meditations on his postlapsarian world. This is, after all, the world of the old Adam and his descendants ("the Victoria Macadamized Road. The old son of Adam gets his name in there too."—*NA,* 5). When Matt climbs an embankment to discover shrubbery, he is reminded of a doorway into "the green garden, the magical lost world of childhood" (*NA,* 8). Nature's "vegetative principle" is found to be "hard at work here to colour over some wound in the earth" (*NA,* 9). Matt meditates on tar, fossils, the "chemical sickness" of wet plaster, the old railway track he discovers, the Domesday Book; and his free-wheeling meditation so preoccupies him that he begins to feel as if he has wandered off the map. He is almost struck by a passing car that blasts its horn like "the trumpet of the archangel" (*NA,* 7). This sound is a prelude, as it were, to his ever-deepening awareness of correspondences between the secular and the sacral.

Everything connects in this book, and the motif of doubled realities is, perhaps, a suggestion that multiplicity of form can yield a single vision and meaning. Just as Proust's *Remembrance of Things Past* begins with a double path that defines two different characters, so also does *A New Athens* begin with doubled forms: a "twinned" trail, two roads, two ruts, two fields, lake and river people, two close girl friends for Matt, two academic streams (Art'n'Ark), and so on. This is not simply Hood's "sportive play of the imagination" but a structure that suggests the kind of mind Matt has—an intelligence that always seeks correspondences, patterns of similarity, duplications.

Matt has an intellect that is provoked by "traces of other forms and

elements of life"—"the turf or the gravel shoulder of the highway or
the bark of trees. Insects, small animals, birdlife, fascinating botani-
cal observations, indications too of the behaviour of the most absorb-
ing of living species" (*NA*, 5). The "layers of resurfacing" on the road
prompt him to wonder "how much past is past," and he speculates
on "some infinite catch-all" or repository for what has once existed
and can never stop existing (*NA*, 11). The continuous connection of
past, present, and future aligns space and time in the novel. Nothing
is fully lost in time, for the "twinned Ontario trail" is perhaps "the
artifact of Bronze Age men" (*NA*, 9), while the embankment he sits
on, though no "access to a new Ur," "no Roman cemetery out of the
pages of Hardy . . . not a new Hadrian's wall designed to exclude
marauding Picts, nor an Indian burying ground" (*NA*, 12), is a link
to the past, for the lettering on one of the upright supports of the
arch over the culvert is a "ghost" script.

   Matt, who plays a little game with topography and botany, is dizzied by "the forms of things" (*NA*, 13). In studying the wild grasses
and flowers, he can see "the pull, the hypnotic fascination that these
proliferating species and sub-species might exert" (*NA*, 15). The
"wild multiplicity of forms" is a "testimony to the communion of the
living and the dead in the great work of science, the classifying of
phenomena and the making sense out of chaotic beauty" (*NA*, 16).
The place begins to "swim and shiver like a slow dissolve" (*NA*, 18),
continuing the hallucinatory effect. As an art historian, Matt does
pioneer research in Loyalist architecture. But so massive is his curiosity that his mind is not restricted by the pastoral tranquillity of
Stoverville and environs or the stone-dwellings of Eastern Ontario.
Matt sees and hears in memory the ghost-train on its last run along
the Stoverville line in 1952. The shining rails no longer exist, having
been sliced into Gilette razor blades ("bits of history unbelievably
sharp"—*NA*, 62), but the past returns as a ritual. Matt hears "the
unmistakable sound of that one special locomotive" with "the flower-
bedecked grand-daughters of the original shareholders presiding over
the pastoral funeral, a weird mechanical 'Lycidas' " (*NA*, 20).

   There is a natural allegorical poetry obtained from local history.
The train sound becomes a pastoral elegy completed by the image of
flowers, "princesses," and melancholy nostalgia. Then there is also an
"abandoned right of way"—a sort of old Adam waywardness, already
hinted at by the McAdamized road. The terminus is Westport, and
suddenly everything leaps into meaning more clearly than before.

   This is documentary fantasy of the doubled realities of fact and fic-

tion. Everything is itself, plus something other. The town Athens is
a vigorous transformation of a small village called Farmersville, and
though the new name sounds pretentious (perhaps derived from
Frances Brooke's vision of "a new Athens rising near the pole"—
NA, 23), the point is not that the place is "as great, as central to
culture as the city of Athena," but only that the schools are "in the
tradition of the Academy, that human culture is continuous, that a
Canadian school two generations removed from the wilderness is the
same kind of school as the Academy, that human nature persists, remains self-identical through many generations of superficial changes"
(*NA*, 59).

The analogy between Canadian and classical worlds is continued in
Matt's identification of Canada with Europe—although, in driving
after a common inheritance, Matt downplays the injustices of Canadian history without altogether removing guilt (*NA*, 60–61). For the
moment his conscience is muffled as he probes "the almost infinite
possibilities of recession"—the fact that in spite of cultural differences
and a history of genocide against our native peoples, "we are all one
family, generation after generation" (*NA*, 43).

The word "generation" is apt, for the book's opening is really a
story of genesis. We are informed how the old road became the new,
how "the history of gravel is the history of metallurgy, of automotive
design, almost indeed of modern society" (*NA*, 6). Matt delves into
the history of Stoverville, carrying us back to the old trains, Loyalist
architecture, and family genealogies. We meet the McGuires and
Sherbournes, and as Matt looks down the corridors of time, he assigns
value to each fact. Nothing is allowed to lie buried and forgotten.
Everything is examined minutely for evidence of the past, because
"we can only apprehend things, lives, by beginning to remember
them" (*NA*, 51). Matt is not an Art'n'Ark historian for nothing.
"New building exists to be transformed into ruin in order that the
meditative human conscience may unearth it," he asserts (*NA*, 51).
And his M.A. study (with old Sylvanus Challies's help) of old stone-
dwellings of Loyalist country is a pioneer contribution to defining a
Canadian style. But the meditative act does not end here. Matt joins
what he discovers in the ground to what he reads in the heavens, so
that architecture is connected to art via a sacred vision. This possibility is first outlined by Maura Boston, the poet-turned-CBC broadcaster. Maura is foil to Matt's first love, Valerie Sherbourne, who
praises Matt for taking the intellectual life seriously (*NA*, 26).

Maura, who was first seen in the short story "Three Halves of a House," has an idea of literature that is sacral and visionary, "derived from long porings over the Book of Revelation, the pages of Blake and, I guess, the writings of Northrop Frye," and in her verse are "many suns, stars, moons, griffins, and sudden illuminations of the Word" (*NA,* 35).

Maura's sacred symbols are a prelude to Mrs. Codrington's visionary art and a subtle preamble to Matt's Revelation, for her sun, moon, star, mythic beasts, and apocalypse are all derived from St. John of Patmos. Perhaps Matt's earliest visionary inspiration is in the connection he makes between the wild flowers and Dürer's studies that showed "the intensity of his concentration" as well as a timeless element when nature mirrors the divine (*NA,* 14–15).

Epiphany is used, as it is often used by Joyce, as a focusing principle. In Hood, epiphany comes to have two contexts—a secular and a sacred—a "sudden flashing forth of intelligibility—aesthetic intelligibility, sometimes intellectual intelligibility" and a manifestation or showing forth of the sacred in the mundane.[33] John Mills has shown how Hood has the facility to draw back "from conventional narrative in order to concentrate on presenting a strong visual image,"[34] and in Chapter 1 Hood uses this technique to suspend "spots of time" in an hallucinatory freeze.

The first epiphany is introduced by a meditation on the "S-shaped" curve that appears repeatedly in nature—"there are inhuman Ss everywhere, the script of the elements" (*NA,* 13)—and in Matt's imagination. Matt goes into a Wordsworthian swoon and hears the ghost-train, as we have already seen. He also has a vision of his future wife, Edie Codrington, who waves at him from the train. Matt thinks of the S-shape: "I saw for minutes more those arms, so slender, so undulant, and I thought they were like wildflowers. Attraction. Why Edie? Arms like grasses" (*NA,* 37). This epiphany is connected to a second one, where Matt actually sees Edie "for the first time" under a green-shaded lamp.

The next three chapters deepen the sacral allegory. Chapter 2, which flashes back fourteen years before the action in Chapter 1, begins on Thanksgiving Day 1952 and develops under the symbol of water. We are given a description of Flora MacLean's boathouse, an ark of sorts (*NA,* 64–65) because it houses Mrs. May-Beth Codrington's painting room. Edie is characterized as a "river girl" or nymph because her "imagination had been formed by her having grown up

on the banks of the St. Lawrence, at first by working carefully along
its shores in canoes and skiffs, with her girlfriends, and later sailing
her own sloop in the local regattas, on one famous occasion capsizing
it as the result of some childish play right out in the middle of the
ship channel" (*NA*, 67). Matt tells us that Edie "spent most of her
childhood and girlhood in and out of, and under, the waters of the
St. Lawrence" (*NA*, 68). And it is now that we see a connection between her way of undulating on the final train from Westport
(*NA*, 80) and water, for the word "undulation" is, in essence, an image of water that suggests a wave of life. Although Matt at this point
still has an amorous relationship with Valerie Sherbourne ("one of the
most virtuous—good-women" he has ever known—*NA*, 71), Edie's
"casual comings-and-goings around the boathouse, her ready use of it
for waterside entertainments of various kinds, her sailboat, the huge
old power cruiser," all combine to reinforce her status in Matt's
imagination as "a princess, a royal, goddess-like, nymphical figurine"
(*NA*, 73). She has great glamour for him and gives him feelings like
those he had faced with the ascendancy of Bea Skaithe in *The Swing
in the Garden*.

Water, in addition to being a dual symbol of regeneration and
chaos, is also a romantic symbol of union. Wordsworth's *The Prelude*
is full of auditory imagery of the sound of moving water, and Matt's
narrative, which digresses in Chapter 1 about the Lake District in
England, echoes Wordsworth's onomatopoeia as it describes the
steady, throbbing, powerful sound of a cruiser on Brown's Bay
(*NA*, 81). In Stoverville "the river overwhelms everything else, and
it is by the river's presence that the place is judged" (*NA*, 104). Matt
even goes on to confess that he's "always glad to sleep by the water,"
for its sound quickly lulls him to sleep (*NA*, 87), and here there is
an obvious link to Wordsworth's connection between the Derwent
and the child sucking at its nurse's breast in *The Prelude:* "Was it for
this/That one, the fairest of all rivers, loved/To blend his murmurs
with my nurse's song . . . ?" Matt quotes from that poem and from
"Three Years She Grew in Sun and Shower" to make explicit Edie's
connection with the river: "And beauty born of murmuring sound/
Shall pass into her face" (*NA*, 104).

The thing about water, as Hood observes, is "that it goes all over
the world. All water is part of one universal system,"[35] so that, as a
symbol, it is an image of enormous depth, especially as it also has a
sacramental significance, and is therefore very relevant to Matt's al-

legory. His wordless proposal to Edie occurs while they are skating on the frozen river, and the dreamy romanticism is so intensified that the moment becomes virtually illusory—"a dream within a dream, reality inside reality inside imagining" (*NA,* 112). Actually, this leads to another epiphany, for the two lovers are given an extraordinary vision of a "ghost-ship," a sunken British gunboat, buried under the "champagne bottle" green ice. It is New Year's Eve and "the light over the green ice" is "powerfully suggestive of festival, even of sacrament." There is a "huge roundel of moon" and the sudden dazzling apparition under the ice grows sharper with starry pinpoints enlarging their concentrated bright coppery shining (*NA,* 113). Nobody else sees the jeweled ghost vessel, so the lovers become the elect by virtue of this "miracle." The "ghost ship" is their special vision, their sacramental ark, and this moment when Edie responds to Matt's unspoken marriage proposal becomes their special covenant of love.

The "ghost ship" scene is a tableau of harmony, and the sunken but transmogrified boat is, as John Mills puts it, "clearly a mandala in its own right imitating, with its perfect proportions, the cosmic harmony which is normally remote from our imaginations and whose essence can be achieved only through art—by the creation of mandalas like this ship or like the work of Mrs. Codrington who, in the first painting which Matt describes, represents the town of Stoverville as though it were a river."[36]

The mandala image is a central one, for even the name "Goderich" has a mandalic significance. As Mrs. Codrington tells Matt, "Goderich" means "God's kingdom," from the Old English *Godes rice,* and when the city of Goderich was first laid out by military engineers, it was arranged in "the shape of a wheel, with a small circular roadway for the hub, and a series of streets running away from the centre like spokes. Seen from above, the centre of town is a perfect wheel"— reminiscent of the prophet's wheel that Ezekiel saw in the middle of the air (*NA,* 105). Mr. Codrington is ever mindful of this mandalic image, and her father had apparently wanted it this way for he had designed a round barn out west, near Regina, with animal stalls built like spokes of a wheel (*NC,* 105).

Given her childhood experience with the mandalic form, it is no surprise to see May-Beth Codrington's deepening interest in other symbolism. She pays attention to names, shapes, and colors, and draws explicit connections among things in the form of doubled realities. Her painting teacher was called Giuseppe Di Angelo, "Joseph

of the Angels," and she picks on Matt's name to connect Old and
New Testaments, old and new dispensations (*NA*, 104). Her picture
of *The Stoverville Annual Regatta* is filled with heraldic colors where
the viewpoint seems to move down the river off Stoverville, from
west to east. The shifting perspective blends space with time, and
forms free associations of images and ideas with such fluency that
there is "a strong feeling of air breathed, air inhaled, or a living atmosphere, and at the same time a distinctly submarine, aqueous
impression, as if the viewer were seeing the town through light reflected off water, maybe even from under water" (*NA*, 109).

The aqueous image converts to fire in Chapter 3. The "ghost ship"
is not forgotten, however, for Chapter 2 ends with the discovery of
a key-shaped rudder (*NA*, 118), and Hood reinforces the religious allegory by this image that serves as a prefiguring of the keys for Mrs.
Codrington's special kingdom—her attic studio—as well as an analogy of other scriptural keys. However, fire comes into the ascendant
in Chapter 3, and it is a pentecostal fire that burns within Mrs. Codrington's sacred art that transfigures reality.

Before he experiences any more of the "fiery" allegorical art of
May-Beth Codrington, Matt first has to purge himself by atoning for
having betrayed his Socialist father's intellectual scruples and his own
wife: the first betrayal is merely hinted at, Hood probably wanting to
signal some later elaboration of this theme, but the second betrayal
occupies a not inconsiderable portion of the chapter. Before she mar-
ries Matt, Edie is required to take religious instruction so that she
can renounce her cradle faith, convert to Catholicism, and have a
church wedding on the feast of Corpus Christi. The venue is Blessed
Sacrament Church, and the Corpus Christi feast is an emblem of a
new bride for Christ, a new member of the Mystical Body.

The marriage centers the chapter in the traditional direction of
comedy, as it is "dominated from the first by those personages from
a thousand romantic farces, the mother of the bride and the father of
the groom, a very funny reversal of usual priorities, the bride's father
and the groom's mama usually being allotted foremost place in such
celebrations" (*NA*, 131). The comedy continues with a brief but hectic honeymoon on a note of hymeneal ecstasy, and the joyful mystery
of marriage ("of how a man shall leave father and mother and cleave
to his wife, and the same in reverse"—*NA*, 142) serves as a prelude
to sorrowful and glorious mysteries to come.

Hood's book shifts perspective but always holds to its religious
thrust. The very opening of Chapter 3, when Mrs. Codrington asks

Matt to identify the signs of the One True Church (*NA*, 119), demonstrates this, and its force continues in Mrs. Codrington's flirtation with Catholic icons—not because of any desire to renounce her own Pentecostal faith, but rather to seek for "imagined signals of heavenly life" (*NA*, 121). After her husband, the trumpet-playing, onetime mayor of Stoverville, dies, she retires from public life to her attic studio and exploits her religious and aesthetic enthusiasm. Her studio is an analogy for the upper chamber where the apostles hid for forty days between Easter and the Ascension, and Mrs. Codrington explains similarities between her situation and that of the apostles. She refers to their incertitude as they awaited the Paraclete, and she mentions the rushing wind and tongues of fire as the Holy Spirit visited them and they began to speak in divers tongues. Her own painting of John Baker Lawson, sometime Mayor of Stoverville, robed as Herod is a startling reminder that art is one of the divers tongues. Matt also sees that her Herod (done as a double study of both famous Herods, father and son) has the fiery red of the tongues of fire (*NA*, 168). Moreover, the dark colors, almost void of luminescence, make it a heavy picture—Dantean in its "menacing, turbulent, almost infernal" atmosphere—and Mrs. Codrington remarks that this suggests "the fires of hell burn without emitting light" (*NA*, 169).

Mrs. Codrington's commitment to sacred art informs the entire second half of Chapter 3 and charges it with a religious *pneuma*. Mrs. Codrington condemns Canadian art for cutting itself off from the world of vision:

> You see, Matthew, the trouble with all this so-called Canadian art, that you meddle about with, is that it's cut off from the world of vision. Group of Seven, group of eight or ten, there's nothing inside them. Emily Carr. Trees and Indians. Nothing for the soul, no footing in the other world for our art. That's a bad thing. The people who paint in this country think that they must go to the majesty of the great outdoors, the world of trees and rocks, of material things, for their subjects. Of course the true subject for the painter is the soul's voyage in the companionship of Jesus and the angels. Rembrandt, Raphael, Michelangelo. A painting should reenact the Redemption and Atonement. (*NA*, 171)

This explains the painting of the two Herods: they were the slayers of innocence (hence the dark red, almost crimson garment in the picture), and they are therefore placed at the center of her sacred art with other actors in the Passion.

Mrs. Codrington's retreat into the upper room does not let the book degenerate into a study of lunacy or eccentricity, but focuses on an heroic pitch of emotion and wisdom that lies behind the transfiguration in sacred art.

The final chapter continues the progression of sorrowful and glorious mysteries to an apocalyptic climax. The 1960s are ushered in with Flora Maclean's death one autumn (*NA,* 180). However, the story continues on an upward spiral. The mystery of the "ghost ship" is pieced together with the aid of Bill Starycz of the Department of Northern Affairs. Matt, having seen the sunken ship in ice, is "one of the elect," "one of the blessed," and his discovery of the rudder is a "key to the whole mystery" (*NA,* 187).

Interestingly, the S-shape motif returns, for the hull design has the *linea serpentina,* "a flat S-curve which recurs again and again in naval architecture in the design of forms that are to be driven through water" (*NA,* 197–98). It is the same line that Matt has seen in the blades of grass and stems of flowers along the abandoned right of way of the Stoverville railway line. And he recognizes it as the line of Edie's arms and shoulders as she sits before her canvas: "The same line and the same undulant turning motion, torsion around an axis, the upward spiralling line of Michelangelo's Sistine Chapel ceiling, the wave of life" (*NA,* 198).

The "wave of life" climbs and spends itself as Mrs. Codrington dies at the end of the summer. She is found seated before a big window, her keys on a table beside her. These keys are another emblem, for they are the keys of death as in Revelation 1:19–20, as well as the keys of a kingdom of sacred art, for they unlock her attic studio. Mrs. Codrington's death liberates Edie's aesthetic impulse, and she paints like she has never painted before: "New anatomies, new figures, new dreams and fantasies" (*NA,* 205). But, paradoxically, the most glorious effect of Mrs. Codrington's death is the revelation of her achievement in visionary art. When Matt discovers the large triptych and gives us his interpretation of it, this is the aesthetic and allegorical climax, for not only is this section a triumphant version of art criticism (whose only rival in fiction is A. M. Klein's brilliant, fevered sequence on the Sistine Chapel in *The Second Scroll*),[37] it is also the major apocalypse in this pilgrimage from joy to sorrow to visionary glory.

Right after New Year's Day, Matt ascends with a locksmith to the "upper regions, burning with impatience" (*NA,* 209). They open the door and soon discover in winter sun the glittering expanses of glass, "round portals like the eyes of God." There on the west wall of the attic is the triptych, which is a continuous, flowing picture entitled *The Population of Stoverville, Ontario, Entering into the New Jerusalem.* The picture is screwed right into the wall, with the screws worked into the narrative of the painting so that they appear in various forms: as jewels in a martyr's crown, apocalyptic stars, nails piercing Christ's hands and feet, clasps on Divine shoes, et cetera. The painting suggests both Ensor's *The Entry of Christ into Brussels* and Stanley Spencer's *Resurrection,* but the "miracle" consists of its ingenious "heavenly inventions" founded on "ordinary life in an ordinary world" (*NA,* 211). The things of this world are given their due, "their line transmitted with utter fidelity," but to the physical world and its "massy definition in space," Mrs. Codrington has given "blurred, swimming symbolic possibilities too, the polarity of Ensor and Spencer" (*NA,* 212). The three panels form a spiral that first moves downward to "the pit of fire and sulphurous smoke, of the second panel," before ascending in Panel III, with the churches, the courthouse, and the city hall all transfigured into a swarming, unified, holy mass before the Blessed Trinity. Graphically within the iconic tradition, the triptych, with its emblems of musical instruments, uncaged birds, white-robed figures, and puffed-up clouds swirling around a heavenly city, appears to be a translation of the Book of Revelation of St. John the Divine. The numbers seven and three play a prominent role in the organization—just as they do in Revelation—and the whole thrust is toward a representation of Christ the God-Man with "His four naked limbs forming the spokes of a holy wheel" (*NA,* 215). This is Christ the King Triumphant, but this is also the sacred mandala that had so dominated Mrs. Codrington's imagination and has now become central in Matt's spiritual life. He himself is in the triptych as the mysterious seventh figure, one of the elect of Stoverville, though his painted face is obscured (*NA,* 216). The other paintings (twelve in number) complete the Codrington collection, which is put on permanent display at the Codrington Colony for the Encouragement of Visionary Art, under the curatorship of Maura Boston, who is inspired to write her greatest poem (in Margaret Avison's manner) on Mrs. Codrington's "upper room." It was the summer exhibition of the collection that had preoccupied Matt at the start of the novel, so now we come full circle. As the book closes, Stoverville is found to have everything—art, music, and theater—for Valerie Sherbourne

and her husband, George Essex, promote religious drama and music,
while the Colony for Visionary Art thrives.

Hood's anagogical method is fully extended in this book, and is
vividly expressed by Mrs. Codrington's theory and art. Through the
final epiphany of her glorious triptych, the visible world of Stoverville
is twined with the world of the spirit into a single metaphysical knot
of atonement and redemption where the damned are cast into perdition while the elect are gathered around the Godhead in the heavenly
city. The new Athens is thereby transfigured into the New Jerusalem,
and Matt, who started out on the road of Old Adam, finds himself
composed into a visionary picture of the heavenly city on top of an
enormous height irradiated by the glory of the Divine. The screws of
the painting fix the vision to the wall, so that now Mrs. Codrington's
keys have a third and triumphant significance: they bear a correspondence to the keys of David (Rev. 6:7–8), for they unlock what
nobody can close again—the upper room with its revelation of the
glorious mystery of redemption.

Reservoir Ravine

In a vital sense, *Reservoir Ravine*[38] is a conceptual extension of *A
New Athens,* because it takes the apocalyptic vision of the holy city in
A New Athens and dresses the new Jerusalem as a beautiful bride,
coming down from God out of Heaven, all dressed for her husband.

Reservoir Ravine is, perhaps, the only instance of a long fiction in
which marriage occupies a central anagogical position. *Tristram
Shandy,* we know, begins with a joke about the hero's conception—
and Hood alludes to this in a humorous, sensual, benign bedroom
scene (*RR,* 231)—but no other fiction (in English, at any rate) has
made marriage and generation the source of its deepest interlocking
relationships and themes. Out of the very context of marriage arise
the issues of contracts, incarnations, and witnesses to time—the very
stuff of human experience, and the existential ground we need to
apprehend.

Marriage, both as sacramental ritual and domestic situation, is of
central importance in this novel, which perhaps more than any previous book by Hood is a very Catholic novel. In *Reservoir Ravine* life
is viewed as a complex recapitulation of the Creation, Fall, and Redemption. The narrative form is curious, related in the third person,
except for Chapter 11, where Matt gives a first-person account of his
gestation and all the things that have made him the sort of person he

now is. Chapter 11 has at least one reference to some event or character from each of the previous ten chapters (for example, his mother's water-stained blue dress; the legend of St. Raphael at the pool of Shiloah; Hal's story of Winnipeg; Miss Saint-Hilaire's sorority; the Great Crash of 1929) and it thereby is a compendium of the type of consciousness Matt now has. Matt, who serves as a witness to his parents' covenant of love, is a Raphael figure, an "affable archangel," who stirs the "waters" of history and finds healing benediction for the products of time that eternity so loves.

Man and woman share equal prominence in this story, where Hood moves away from Stoverville and its environs and back to Toronto, the locale of the first novel in the series. The central characters are Matt's parents, who first meet each other in the mid-1920s, "arguably the most exciting and transformative years of the century" (*RR*, 12). Chapter 1 is Isabelle Archambault's, whereas Chapter 2 introduces us to her husband-to-be, Andrew Goderich. Isabelle rises to the fore in Chapter 3, shares a "mad revel" with Andrew in Chapter 4, and dominates Chapter 5 with its focal imagery of water and her lavender blue evening dress. After Hal Forbes's disturbing Winnipeg story in Chapter 6—a crucially important subnarrative—she accepts Andrew's wordless marriage proposal in Chapter 7. The next part is a commemoration of their nuptials and honeymoon, and after this, it is Andrew's turn to come to the fore with his ambitious exploration of theories of value and conceptual thought. Andrew, however, does not displace Isabelle; it is simply that, during her pregnancies, Isabelle settles into impending motherhood with the contentment of one whose freedom is enriched rather than compromised or limited. The final two chapters are her son's, as he plays his Raphael role—that of a healing wonderworker, innocent but fundamentally good, comforting old, blind Isabelle and serving as important witness to his parents' love and the *Zeitgeist* of Canada prior to the 1970s.

The idea of a witness (whether a sacred or secular one) is important in this novel, which seeks to study the national character through the narrator's personal pantheon of remembered figures from his past. Matt's memories make the past incarnate: the word becomes flesh as these remembered figures exist prismatically "under several aspects and many lights" in Matt's "slowly maturing body of revealed truth" (*RR*, 202). Some of these figures Matt has never met in person, but through his parents' testimonies they burst into being and are bound together in "a system of *correspondences,* a tough network of analogies and nerves, cutting much deeper than mere similarity, and binding all of being together in a continually sliding, self-adjusting set of relations supported by the underlying familiarity of all existence" (*RR*, 204).

The generational theme thrusts subtly toward the motif of witness. The first state of nature is existence or being; but beings have this in common with one another—that, "supported in being," they thrust toward being "more and more fully" (*RR*, 204). Matt believes that "every possible mode of being exists in the mind of God," and, therefore, all being offers witness to Him, the divine ground of our existence or nativity. As Matt says, "the act of bearing evidence, of giving testimony, of refusing to bear false witness is a sacred act, a holy act" (*RR*, 207).

The first witness is Isabelle, who in 1921 (the start of the story) is a brilliant school graduate, "a young person of an independent turn of mind," with ten firsts in her final exams. Docile, sweet, slender, graceful, energetic, and healthy, she is a veritable compendium of physical, intellectual, and moral virtues. Cuddly to look at, and "pet" of her convent-school, she has "calm, composure and inward glee" (*RR*, 7)—a balance of qualities that idealize her character. She is not goody-goody or ethereal: she is very much of her world—the young lady walking about town and striving to be the New Woman. "Fires" are "banked in this cuddly girl" (*RR*, 7) who hates corsets, bobs her hair, shortens her hem, and wears a bra long before these become the fashion of Victorian society in Toronto. Hood portrays her without condescension. Just like Edie or May-Beth Codrington in *A New Athens*, Isabelle has an autonomy that permits her to say and do things that go against the grain of male-chauvinist society. Her intellectual distinction is genuine, and she goes on to University College and later, in a melodramatic but exciting episode, crashes the all-male sanctum of Hart House, where, disguised as a young man, she creates an uproar.

Isabelle's moral fiber is tested early. When she gets a bank job at the Domestic and Foreign Bank of Upper Canada, she has to resist the advances of an old roué, Colonel Jarvis (a detestable colonial), and his procurer, Chastel Baby (the "last of a perfectly genuine, though drastically etiolated-ashen-stock, of a family so ancient in Toronto terms as to have its roots in Eden"—*RR*, 62). The two seducers are the personification of temptation and drawn like Dickensian caricatures, right from their names to their evil as they leer at Isabelle and insinuate pleasures of the flesh available in their fourth-floor "seraglio" (*RR*, 67).

Isabelle's virtue is supported by the guardianship of "indestructible and unsinkable" Miss Emily Saint-Hilaire (*RR*, 66), secretarial supervisor at the bank, and owner of a large boarding-house on Summerhill Gardens "lying just below the reservoir" (*RR*, 15). Miss Saint-Hilaire (whose surname, derived from Hilary, suggests a cheerful protectress) is caricatured as a Mother Superior in charge of a cloister. Her boarding-house is a "scented, protected world, sororal, safe" (*RR*, 68), and even her domain at the bank is run according to "her notions of politeness and good behaviour" (*RR*, 66).

On the male side, Andrew Goderich as junior university lecturer at the University of Toronto is introduced by Professor Brett, Chairman of Philosophy, to an older guardian angel in the form of Reb Samuel Aaronsohn, a senior lecturer, expert in the metaphysics of ethics, philosophy of religion, and phenomenological historiography. Aaronsohn (etymologically derived from the Hebrew for "lofty mountaineer") has pontifical gravity and wisdom as he comes to Canada to stand off from his German homeland for a few years "in order to make some sort of reassessment of her nature as a religious and secular community" (*RR*, 35). He tries to read a pattern that will do justice to his idea of history as the fulfillment in time of an eternal vision of redemption. Where Miss Sainte-Hilaire may be seen as a woman doing battle against male chauvinism and lechery, Rabbi Aaronsohn can be viewed as a "military philosopher"—a sly cross-reference to the title of a novel by Anthony Powell, but, more appropriately, a label for this onetime soldier, wounded in battle, and now an extraordinary philosopher (*RR*, 36).

As Isabelle tries to develop herself in the vanguard of the New Woman, young Andrew Goderich, with an M.A. from McGill in ethics, employs his "natural inquisitiveness" (*RR*, 34) to develop a theory of axiology that will ultimately reconcile the material and the spiritual. With Professor Brett's assistance, he starts his university career at the top of the philosophical stairs (*RR*, 50)—an elevation that is more than simply a figure of speech. Aaronsohn, eleven years older and wiser, is loftier in intellectual stature, but Andrew comes under his aegis and learns to make vital analogies between secular and salvation history.

Chapters 3 and 4 intertwine the futures of Isabelle and Andrew. Hood, so good at satirizing the concupiscence of Colonel Jarvis and

the immoral collaboration of Chastel Baby, also excels in romanticism, and he sketches wonderfully the stars in Isabelle's eyes as she
falls in love with Andrew. The lovers' first shared passion appears to
be intellectual. At an important political debate on the League of
Nations in Hart House, with the illustrious Arthur Balfour in at-
tendance, Isabelle attains a certain notoriety by disguising herself as
a male, sneaking into the all-male sanctum, and then rising to de-
clare her impassioned support of a young history don who argues for
the union of heavenly and earthly cities, a "double Jerusalem," with
the Leagues seen as the several tribes of Israel, and the world community as the communion of mankind (*RR,* 56–57).

This episode (with its imitations of erudite academic debate) is of
crucial importance in the book, not simply because it glorifies Isabelle or draws her closer to Andrew, but because it connects the secular and the sacral as a set of Swedenborgian correspondences. To begin with, the presence of Earl Balfour, Renaissance man "with an
extraordinary richness of wit and judgment" (*RR,* 48), yields yet another guardian figure. Balfour, preoccupied with the Zionist question
and utterly convinced of the immeasurable debt owed to Judaism by
Christianity and Western civilization, is a witness to history on a
world scale. His Zionism is not simply a stark political concept, but
a religious idea that links up with the young history don's argument
that "the Holy Land *is* in Manitoba and in Quebec, and it is the other
way around too" (*RR,* 55). This echoes the analogy between the new
Athens and the New Jerusalem in Mrs. Codrington's visionary art,
and it anticipates Andrew's theology of politics. Moreover, it attests
to the pattern of doubled realities in Hood's work, and even heralds
the theme of holocaust that germinates later.

Balfour's presence, then, like Maritain's in *The Swing in the Garden,*
heightens the documentary fantasy and deepens the didacticism while
balancing the novel and history. In following the romance and marriage of Isabelle and Andrew, the novel is ever mindful of the world
background, and the story becomes not simply a family or marital
history, but the objectification of being on a universal scale. After all,
the financial crash of 1929 is not simply a North American catastrophe, but the very image of a calamitous fall from grace. As Andrew
declares, it is the end of the world, the end of something (*RR,* 224).
He later posits money as an emblem of our faith in society (*RR,* 227),
and the failure of money marks the disintegration of a set of values.
The earlier burning of the bank's paper money is Jarvis's "fall from

grace," whereby he goes into a Dantean descent (*RR*, 64–65). The explosive Manitoba labor situation is a model of growing universal restlessness and anarchy, and the burning tramcar and riotous violence symbolize a world going up in flames.

Interestingly, the bank's collapse incarnates two contrary ideas. The ritualistic burning of the paper money mixes classical and Christian religious imagery and provides a social mythology for Canada. There is a Friday inferno, a festive saturnalia or "mad revel" (*RR*, 76), where the human witnesses (including Isabelle and her suitor, Andrew) descend "to the lowest depths of the furnace room, lighted only by eternally blazing arc lamps and the glowing eyes of the furnace" (*RR*, 74). Fires are prepared and, after Isabelle is invited to roll in the mound of money, the paper is burned. Hood's lyrical description becomes intensely poetic and apocalyptic, as it presages the ghastly holocaust to come in Nazi Germany, but there is a mad beauty and purity in the scene as Andrew sees in the instant that he loves Isabelle (*RR*, 77). Their mutual, unspoken love is a real presence burning with the inferno, and although there are tones of mockery in the "motley" look on Andrew's face and the burning paper wealth, Hood is quite serious about the zeal of love.

The romantic mode continues in Chapter 5 with light satire on Isabelle's lingerie (*RR*, 84) and the emblem of the lavender blue evening dress. This dress adds to the gently perfumed romance, but it becomes a very significant emblem of the waters of memory, whose widening ripples stir historical associations among Isabelle, her ancestors, and progeny. To begin with, the fabric is a gift from her great-great-aunt Lil, whose husband was once the *soi-disant* friend of Richard Strauss (*RR*, 78). So, the dress establishes a link between Isabelle and her progenitors, and through them, a link between epochs, the famous Strauss becoming a part of Isabelle's family mythology. The dress is completed in the spring, and, in this way, becomes a new garment—a baptismal emblem. This symbolic association is emphasized by a humorous incident at the Island Aquatic Club, when Isabelle is splashed by Andrew in the presence of his rival-suitor, the gawky westerner Hal Forbes. Water imagery becomes strong in this section: the blue silk dress ripples and changes with Isabelle's movement (*RR*, 83); the young lovers dance at "the Aquatic" (*RR*, 83); and Isabelle, compared to a "nymph" in Pope's satire (*RR*, 84), is splashed by Andrew, as Hal, her other suitor, rolls on his back in the lagoon (*RR*, 96). All these aqueous images are an essential part of the

Raphael myth that subtly shapes the book by showing how the waters
of memory can be stirred, generation by generation, that we might
miraculously see our own reflections in our ancestors' past.

The romance passes over water and through fire and ice. We have
already seen the near baptism by water in the lagoon, and the satur-
nalian holocaust of the paper money. The love of Isabelle and Andrew
crystallizes into a wordless marriage proposal during their visit to Hal
Forbes's ice-house. Hal, an ice and fuel salesman (and, therefore, an
agent in fundamental matters of life), invites the couple to the ice-
house, "an enchanted ice palace" (RR, 125). The "magical sunny cave
of ice" (RR, 126) is like the interior of an iceberg, and the rainbow
colors within the ghostly labyrinth give the lovers the impression of
their being imprisoned inside a diamond (RR, 129). The magic of the
phenomenon is somewhat reminiscent of the beautiful epiphany of the
"ghost ship" under ice in A New Athens, and here, as in that novel,
the lovers move toward a betrothal. Andrew is not actually heard to
say anything, but Hal, who is "a bit in awe" of him (RR, 125), does
see the lovers' forms swim together and merge, closer and closer.
Then he overhears Isabelle (whose enchanting being has its own "fire
and ice" quality—RR, 117) utter words that are really an acceptance
of a marriage proposal, and he becomes in this rainbow-colored moment a witness to the arc of their love-covenant (RR, 129).

It is at this point that the sacrament of matrimony begins to take
hold in the novel, as Andrew finds himself participating in a French
nuptial rite because his bride comes from a French Canadian family. The linguistic comedy, where Andrew deciphers the unfamiliar
French phrases by putting them into the conventional Latin of orthodox Catholicism (RR, 130), does not displace or blur the impressive
beauty and passion of the religious ceremony, or the spiritual implications of a sacrament which requires man and woman to be mutual
gifts to each other, "without reservation of self" (RR, 130).

The marriage ceremony becomes a didactic emblem that deepens
the analogy between human union and the marriage of Christ and the
Church. Marriage is theologically held to be the very first example of
human society, and especially of a society that has not been destroyed
by Original Sin (RR, 133). Marriage is celebrated often in the Bible,
particularly in the Book of Tobit (where Raphael the archangel figures prominently as witness and thaumaturge), the Song of Solomon,
and the Gospels where Christ works a great miracle at the marriage-

feast of Cana. Consequently, the wedding in *Reservoir Ravine* has strong associations with both old and new scriptural orders.

There is a vibrant wedding breakfast, which Aaronsohn attends after avoiding the church ceremony, and the mutual celebration of Andrew and Aaronsohn echoes "something Biblical, something Jewish" (*RR,* 137). The wedding joy is extended by a deep enthusiasm in the meditations of the two friends during the nuptial mass and the party. These reflections on fundamental concepts are not perverse digressions or indulgences, but complex ways of filtering out the existential ground of man. During the church ceremony, Andrew meditates on the nature and ground of concepts: "The human self a nature which wrenches value into concept. To think is to evaluate. No, the other way around. To be valuable will be to exist as issuing in concept; to evaluate will be to form concepts" (*RR,* 136). Later, Aaronsohn argues that "we can only form concepts because God IS AS HE IS," which means that the concept is "the human, incarnate, means of apprehension of the existential ground" (*RR,* 136). And marriage, by its emphasis on the primacy of generation as a role in the married state, becomes the means to make the word flesh, or, in other words, to make human or incarnate being that by its multiplication can magnify God.

Aaronsohn's presence at the wedding feast is not just a convenient way for Hood to launch into a heavily philosophical meditation. It manifests the author's deep personal conviction that Christianity and Jewry are witnesses to each other. Andrew, founding his argument on the nature of the Mystical Body of Christ, asserts that Catholics are at one with Jews (*RR,* 158), a view that is a perfect reflection of Hood's own belief that "we are all Jews, just as we are all Greeks, so far as we share in the historical mission of Jewry" (*GB,* 139). When Andrew goes on to describe Canada as a nation founded on a religious idea (*RR,* 154), he echoes not only the history don in the Hart House debate, but all those theologians who draw an analogy between the world and the dispersed tribes of Israel, or between politics and religion.

Aaronsohn, who is "almost a saint," has studied the problem of good and evil "as deeply as any man can" (*RR,* 119). He serves as a form of conscience, not simply because of his criticism of the increasing decadence in European politics but because he stimulates Andrew with significant ideas about ethics and epistemology. When he sets to completing his book, *The Place of Conceptual Thought in Ethical Judgments*, Andrew revises his draft according to what he has learned from Aaronsohn (*RR*, 125), and although Aaronsohn's return to Germany in the 1930s marks the decline and cessation of correspondence between the two friends, Andrew's immersion in the "deep waters" of theology and politics (*RR*, 158) never does change into a dry spell of intellectual sterility. Instead, his life continues as a perpetual commitment to ideas of virtue and to actions that fulfill those ideas. He is characterized as the first philosopher ever to use the term "existential" before it became a common label in European philosophy (*RR*, 151), and his life becomes a witness to those values that make us honorable.

Andrew is a witness to Aaronsohn's quest after a just evaluation of the course of history. Unlike most Torontonians of his era, who do not socialize freely with Jews (*RR*, 55), Andrew becomes a close friend of a Jewish scholar who even dances at his wedding. Andrew continually identifies with Jews: "A Christian *is* a Jew; he must be. And the more he comprehends his Christianity, whether by the light of Faith or merely by reason, the more a Jew he becomes" (*RR*, 50). This is not exactly a revolutionary idea, for in Catholic theology a Christian is spiritually a Jew, being a follower of Christ, Himself a Jew. Andrew's friendship with Aaronsohn has more than a tinge of gentle sadness and foreboding, for as Aaronsohn returns to Germany, we anticipate the irreversibly tragic course of the Holocaust and its mad, voracious fires. The impending world war is a recapitulation of the fall of man, and there is little comfort to be derived from the North American mood of industrial progress and prosperity which creates a false Eden filled with automobiles (*RR*, 156). Perhaps, the car wheels (which also figure, as we have seen, in *The Swing in the Garden*), are a subtle symbol of the momentum with which man propels himself out of Eden!

Actually, Andrew becomes a major moral witness to the world as well through his wavering friendship with Hal Forbes, the mysterious stranger from the West, who is really no stranger in the New Age fiction, having been the one who saved young Matt from drowning in *The Swing in the Garden*, and having also been Ishy's suitor before Andrew Goderich arrived on the scene. Close to the middle of the novel, Hal's eyewitness account of the great Winnipeg Strike and riot of 1919 quickens our interest in Canadian politics of the period. Hal's chronicle of his father's victimization in the metal trade is filled with a sense of violent and ugly labor problems—a parallel to proletarian unrest in Czarist Russia (*RR,* 107, 112), and serves as an indictment of social injustice. Hal's memories of J. S. Woodsworth stir Andrew's interest in the concept of justice. Woodsworth was a radical political thinker who set moral guidelines for all Canadians and issued grave warnings about social injustice,[39] and Hal's memories confirm Andrew's feelings that Canada has to right itself and clear its conscience.

Injustice, a predominant theme in Hood's fiction, is made incarnate in *Reservoir Ravine.* Andrew's father writes from Barringford, Nova Scotia, in 1927 about the injustice he has suffered. A barrister and magistrate, Anthony Augustus Goderich believes thoroughly in the practice of law and the impartial execution of the local magistracy, and he is, therefore, beyond party politics or party discipline. Consequently, he is deprived of higher appointments, and in his middle years he becomes a discontented man, as his plaintive letter to Andrew shows (*RR,* 161–62). Andrew's mission is to study these things and then try and work out his ideas in the flesh. He is a Nativity figure who argues that justice implies a clear conscience—a very Canadian thing, to his mind, and to Aaronsohn's as well:

"The political conception of Canada is essentially religious, and Jewish or at the least Judeo-Christian," conceded Aaronsohn. "It is the difference between Canada and the United States. The political idea of America was from its beginnings secular; the Whig notion of liberty as obtaining between contracting parties, the Lockeian idea of property and contract lies beneath the American union and American liberty. But the Canadian union is animated—if at all—by religious morality, by the notion that the great differences which separate peoples, in fact the greatest—language, religion, race—can be mitigated or overcome by virtue under law. To be a Canadian in act is a guarantee of a good conscience."

"You can't be wholly Canadian without a clear conscience," said Andrew, "and this is true of humanity in general. You can't be wholly a man without a clear conscience."

"I think you must claim that Canadianism is the seeing-of-man-as-religiously-political." (*RR,* 154)

These stirring words (reminiscent of Roger Talbot's view in *A Game of Touch*) are idealistic wish-fulfillment, not yet vindicated by contemporary Canadian politics and morals, but they are, undoubtedly, magnificently magnanimous.

The novel enters its Nativity and Redemption phases. After a witty hymeneal exaltation of love on Lake Ontario, where the steamer and honeymooners turn out to be carnal replicas of the wedding-cake and its miniature wedding couple (*RR*, 139–40), Andrew and Isabelle turn to fulfilling the procreative function of marriage. Amanda Louise's birth in October 1927 is an objectification of being, and the Christmas spirit soon follows, with its heraldic symbols of the Nativity: red for the Sacred Heart and its blood; green for nature and hope; and white for illumination and belief (*RR*, 204). With Matt's appearance on the scene—his conception and birth frame the novel—the procession and products of time are clarified.

Matt sees in the Christmas gifts and wrappings—especially his mother's hatbox and its designs—an emblem of the variables and repetitions of existence. The repeated diagonal patterns incite obsessive behavior: "the counting, recounting, attempting to calculate how many variables are found in the illustration—how existence is to be hedged" (*RR*, 183). The magnificent advertising art of the 1920s appeals to his senses and stirs his analytic faculty, and Matt's recognition of patterns confers values on time.

This is similar to his adoration of his mother's lavender blue evening-dress, and crystallizes his view that there is "no separation, chasm, gulf," between what had been going on before he was born and what is happening now. The "liquid colouring of the silk" makes the dress seem "watered silk" in a very literal way. Matt knows of his mother's near-immersion and the water stains, part of his parents' "homemade anthology of family folk-lore," cause profound feeling, "a complex mixed mash of raw emotion, and raw perception," to "well up" within him (*RR*, 190–91). Matt learns how history is prepared for us by our predecessors and that there is really no gulf between us and them, for time is a continuum objectified in being:

When Andrew dangled Ishy out over the water and threatened to let go, while Hal Forbes lay on his back, fully clothed, in the cooling waters of Long Pond, spouting now and then like a whale and refusing to be rescued, accusing Andrew from a distance of having tried to drown him, all three, plus the hilarious crowd of onlooking dancers, were preparing my history for me. When in the wet bright spring of 1937, Mr. Forbes saved me from drowning, as I now believe he did, in an extension of the epos which in its turn became liturgically authentic, he merely added a kind of continuous commentary, a footnote, to the other part of the legend. Now I learn, decades later, that Mr. Forbes and "Hal from the 'peg' " are one and the same, which I couldn't claim to have understood consciously at the age of seven when Mr. Forbes yanked me out of the full crater in the vacant lot, a peculiar act of midwifery strangely evoking a new birth. (*RR*, 191–92)

Such reflective passages show how Hood exploits Wordsworthian "spots of time" and an inner temporal music:

The whole of being is conserved together, as it seems to me, and parts of it are allowed to fall into time at different points, somewhat as an inner voice in a counterpointed structure can be created on the piano in an apparently almost random sequence of struck keys, invisible, inaudible, in the notes on the page, but visible, audible, intelligible, when struck. The inner voice is planned and given in the music though the mere notes conceal it.

Intelligible utterance dropped into the undifferentiated sequence of time: that seems to be what being is. In the beginning was the Word and the Word was with God and the Word was God. We are all, every one of us at any time, the precursor and the evangelist too, both John, in for the beginning, in for the end. (*RR*, 192)

The Nativity phase is gloriously emphatic, as Matt celebrates the insight that "we're the prizes our grandparents prepare in prophecy, our parents take in action. Our natures begin long before conception. There is clearly some sense in which they have no earthly beginning, or the same extremely qualified beginning that history has. BANG" (*RR*, 192). As Blake has said, "Eternity is in love with the productions of time,"[40] and Matt extends the idea to encompass the whole of history as being that which is known from Eternity by the Eternal "which loves the productions of time and prepares what time reveals" (*RR*, 193).

Matt sees how "all the way through the nineteen-twenties" his "poor small existence was being gathered together by creative might, being prepared by courtship and love" (*RR*, 195). His existence was also being prepared by family inheritance and national character. Though conceived around the beginning of August 1929 and born at the end of April 1930, Matt is connected to the Crash of 1929, just as he is connected to the lagoon splashing, the Winnipeg General Strike, and two World Wars.

The insistence on generalized, apocalyptic links makes Hood's book a weighty fiction that continuously expands its meanings. The final two chapters complete the analogical form of the fiction and give further elevation to Hood's stature as an allegorist. As Matt moves his own figure into the narrative, we become increasingly aware of his role as a Raphael symbol in a myth of Redemption. The "affable archangel," as Milton called him in *Paradise Lost* (Bk. VII, 1. 41), is a miraculous guardian and witness in *The Book of Tobit,* a didactic work which, among other things, shows a concern for marriage, justice, and charity. Raphael leads Tobias to a happy marriage with Sarah, collects Tobias' inheritance as a wedding gift, and finally brings the happy couple back to Tobit, whose blindness he cures. Before returning to the heavenly court, he reveals himself to be one of the Seven Angels, who are ever ready to enter into the presence of the Lord's glory. Raphael is the elect—someone called upon to carry out a special task—and he uses holy water in his exorcisms, suggesting to us that he could be the "angel of the Lord" who at intervals comes down to the pool, stirs the waters, and heals the sick who use the waters (John 5:1–5).[41]

With this scriptural paradigm in mind, it now becomes easy for us to perceive Hood's allegorical design for Matt. We have already seen how central and significant an event the ceremony of marriage is in *Reservoir Ravine,* and when we recall Isabelle's blue evening-dress and hat-box, we find two material gifts that are important epiphanous inheritances to Matt. The ideas of a contract and witness also function importantly in Hood's fiction, just as they do in *Tobit.* The marriage contract is an analogy for the covenant between Christ and the Church, and there is also a metaphorical contract between Canada and Jerusalem. We have also seen how various witnesses testify to the history of the period—Hal, Aaronsohn, Miss Sainte-Hilaire, Professor Brett, Colonel Jarvis, et cetera—but the final human witness is Matt himself, already cast as one of the elect in *A New Athens.* Matt's special task is to synthesize history and to reconcile the human with the divine. In *The Swing in the Garden,* he makes history a vast reservoir into which he dips frequently, and, of course, it is Hood's intention to have Matt dipping into this reservoir all through the *roman fleuve.*

In *A New Athens,* Matt's Janus-headed historical role is defined clearly as he follows the footpaths of the divine in the corridors of history, and now, in *Reservoir Ravine,* he turns once more to the reservoir as a form of memory, a natural symbol of his own psyche and an emblem of moral imagination, in order to stir the waters of every decade in his parents' story. Hence the abundance of water imagery and Matt's early memory of being wheeled around the paths of the ravine to the "wide, placid, open circle of shining water" (*RR,* 197).

At the end of the text, he is about to voyage to "terra incognita" (*RR,* 238). As his mother grows old and blind, and sits by her window at St. Raphael's nursing home (*RR,* 222), Matt visits her and comforts her. He is now her "eyes," because it is his mission to see for her and for all of us in order to discover a moral pattern in our national life and in the unfolding of the world.

At the end of the book, the world of his parents has changed. Reports of German decadence show how the grip of reason is breaking (*RR,* 231). Germany is on the brink of a new order, but there are omens of world catastrophe, and philosophy is losing its way. If Matt were to express this world by artistic referents, he would not conjure up Giorgione, Titian, Tiepolo, Spenser, Ensor, Dürer, or Hopper any more; he might, instead, turn to Goya or Munch or Picasso. But Matt does not think primarily of art—at least not in a purely secular way. He is a healing witness to history, an antiquary who can love old things just as he can accept change, because he places his faith in the fundamental benevolent impulses of man, who is part angel no less than he is part animal.

Although the Toronto reservoir is filled over, Matt has his reservoir of memory. It is to his credit as an encyclopedist of his age that he can look into his reservoir and find a meaning for his life within a divine scheme. As a witness to his parents, as a critic of his own age, Matt is creator and redeemer: he gathers out of "the undifferentiated manifold of time of spouts, points, upwellings of persons" a personal and national myth of Nativity, Fall, and Redemption, and, in this way, he exists in the creative impulse of God, who knows what Matt is still to become in his uncompleted life.

Chapter Eight
Conclusion

The inner form of the New Age series recognizes the dangers that arise from the fundamentally abstract nature of the novel as outlined by Lukács: "the risk of overlapping into lyricism or drama, the risk of sinking to the level of mere entertainment literature."[1] Hood triumphs over these risks by signaling clearly all that lies outside and beyond the particular confines of the world. In this sense, he is at once at odds with Balzacian period melodrama as he is with Robbe-Grillet's objectivity, two extremes of realist fiction.

Hood also resists the anxiety-neurosis of Canadian fiction and other negative attitudes that have colored most of twentieth-century fiction. For him, the creation of forms is not a confirmation of dissonance, as the ironic view of literature would have it, but, rather, a confirmation of a divine consonance that makes and remakes being as a perpetual process of generated beauty and wholeness. However, his resistance to the negative raises a question of the fullness of his epical vision, because we wonder if life can be truthfully rendered in art without a problematic individual or a sense of evil.

The question is resolved when we turn and look back upon the totality of his work. Only theodicy can account for all the evil in the world, so Hood's fiction expresses only those evils that allow for remedy, taking the medieval world-view that the Creator in His design has a stake in the Earth and uses the earthly city as a staging ground for salvation. Evil in Hood is a crucial experience not of itself but of the sacred. In *The Fruit Man, The Meat Man & The Manager* and *Dark Glasses,* in particular, the penitential theme and the language of confession bring to light human blindness, equivocation, and scandalousness. Evil here is still embedded in the matrix of emotion, and this passionate note gives rise to objectification. The confessionalism and penance (as in "Dark Glasses" or "Whos Paying for this Call") push to the outside the emotion which would otherwise be shut up in itself as an impression of the soul. Through confession and apocalyptic emblem the consciousness of fault is brought into the light of speech and becomes an experience of man's own absurdity, suffering, and incapacity.

Evil becomes particularized as sin which makes a character incomprehensible to himself. God is hidden, the human will impaired by a ritualistic bondage to habit (as in "Paradise Retained?") or to material self-gratification (as in "God Has Manifested Himself As Canadian Tire"). Hood appears to substantiate Paul Ricoeur's concepts of sin, frequently giving us characters who miss their targets, follow tortuous roads, and remain stiff-necked with revolt, pride, envy, possessiveness, or folly.[2]

Hood objectifies sin as transgression, especially when he tackles the idea of justice in many of his short stories and in all of his novels. By making justice a religious concept, he equates injustice with impiety in the profane earthly city. *You Cant Get There From Here* is, perhaps, the most vividly convincing example of this, where greed, selfishness, envy, and betrayal become perdition itself. Jedeb lacks the scrupulous conscience required to meditate and act upon the problem; his eyes are enlightened only when the situation is beyond repair.

The entire form of Hood's fiction is perceived clearly because it is so strongly moral. *None Genuine Without This Signature* collects the signatures of social evils, those very acts that crush our spirit in striving after illusory powers. In "God Has Manifested Himself As Canadian Tire" our society is satirized because of its naive perception of comfort and happiness. The Canadian Tire catalog is not simply a consumer's aid. It is an emblem of the modern century's redoubled efforts to make everyone a satisfied consumer who will live in an effortless world. Civilization is reduced to a spiritless sense of institutions, products, and momentum. Man becomes the owning animal, dwarfed, however, by the substitutes for community. The story confirms Ernest Becker's view that "the self-display of consumer man is perhaps the emptiest agonism of all historical time, and certainly the loneliest."[3]

Hood's moral sense informs all his fiction, but it is often so subtle that we miss its involvement with evil. The "small cave of fact" in the satirical "Breaking Off," for instance, is a comic symbol of the Leviathan growth of illusory efficiency. The wild duplication of paper at the photocopying center is the sign of a mechanical monstrousness. Man reproduces the products of his time without creating any aesthetic object of lasting significance. He is simply consumed by his own profligate appetite.

The immense vitality in Hood's fiction, the numerous games his characters play, the many jobs they perform, are all checks to the sense of evil. The world comes alive in touch football, hockey, kite-flying, swimming, wrestling, music, art, fruit-pulping, debating, boat-building, bicycling, hiking, politics. The sense of play and games merges quite naturally with the concept of holiness—just as it does in Johan Huizinga's *Homo ludens*. Hood's individuals are often living embodiments of what Huizinga calls *Homo poeta,* Man the Creator of Meaning.[4] There is a sense of awe in man's play, for his games are often expressions of the strong bonds of communality and brotherhood. Their creative energies lure us and enlarge our spirit. Games and art relieve evil, by giving us the freedom to leave records of human purpose.

But the creation of meaning (whether through holiness, rapt meditation, work, historical synthesis, visionary art) is something which can be achieved only through an interaction with the world. And this interaction produces a problematic individual. As Lukács phrases it, "the contingent world and the problematic individual are realities which mutually determine one another. If the individual is unproblematic, then his aims are given to him with immediate obviousness, and the realisation of the world constructed by these given aims may involve hindrances and difficulties but never any serious threat to his interior life."[5] Is this so with Matt Goderich? Only on the surface, for Matt's life is a series of examined, although largely unresolved, problems of being. Although sometimes "a bit of a pompous ass," he is fundamentally "innocent and good"—as May-Beth Codrington recognizes (*NA,* 172). He does not suffer the way a Raskolnikov or Leopold Bloom or Mohun Biswas suffers, but this is only because he adapts the discrete, unlimited nature of the material of life to the infinity of God's meaning. His limitation as a character is his faith, which is really a paradox, because where his biography is subjective and constrained by his possible experiences, his faith permits larger possibilities outside his immediate world. It is a special paradox, a Dantean one, where the beginning and end take place between two points in eternity: generation (and its chaos that he seeks to order) and the certainty of redemption.

Hood's epical fiction is a reading of the Book of Life according to the Book of Divine Revelation. The world is a real one—not an illusion. Dense with detail, thick with fact, it is flawed but redeemable; and the epical hero, Matt Goderich, is far from lonely, for he is a bearer not only of his own destiny, but of a gospel for all mankind. Instead of romantic disillusionment, Hood offers us the superrealism of one who can see where God is to be found in a world that believes God is dead or indifferent. For a writer who, by his own avowal, detests irony, this might well be Hood's supreme irony. Hood is an original—the first and only meditative writer in Canadian fiction who by his anagogical approach and transcendental allegory conditions the novel toward the paramount significance of human experience.

Notes and References

Preface

1. Northrop Frye, *Anatomy of Criticism* (Princeton: Princeton University Press, 1973), p. 89.

Chapter One

1. Hugh Hood, "Before the Flood," in *Before The Flood,* J. R. (Tim) Struthers (Downsview: ECW Press, 1979), p. 12. All quotations are from this edition.
2. Hugh Hood, "The Governor's Bridge Is Closed," in *The Governor's Bridge Is Closed* (Ottawa, 1973), p. 12. All quotations are from this edition and are denoted by *GB* in the text.
3. J. R. (Tim) Struthers, "An Interview with Hugh Hood," in *Before The Flood,* p. 31.
4. Hood, "Before the Flood," pp. 5–20.
5. Ibid., p. 5.
6. Ibid., p. 7.
7. Ibid., pp. 9–10.
8. Ibid., p. 10.
9. Ibid., p. 11.
10. Ibid., p. 12.
11. Ibid., p. 14.
12. Ibid.
13. Struthers, "An Interview with Hugh Hood," pp. 22–23.
14. Ibid., p. 49.
15. Linda Sandler, "Near Proust And Yonge," *Books in Canada,* December 1975, p. 6.
16. Hugh Hood, letter to Naim Kattan, *Le Devoir,* 12 December 1964, p. 15.
17. Hugh Hood, "The End of It," in *Flying a Red Kite* (Toronto, 1962), pp. 218–39.
18. Robert Fulford, "Hugh Hood's Misused Talent," *Toronto Star,* 11 October 1967, p. 43.
19. Frank Davey, *From There to Here* (Erin, Ontario: Press Porcepic, 1974), p. 138.
20. William H. New, "14: Fiction," in *Literary History of Canada,* ed. Carl F. Klinck, 2d ed. (Toronto: University of Toronto Press, 1976), 3:264.

21. John Moss, *Sex and Violence in the Canadian Novel* (Toronto, 1977), p. 235.

22. Patricia Morley, "Where the Myth Touches Us," review of *The Swing in the Garden. Canadian Literature,* no. 67 (Winter 1976):99.

23. George Woodcock, "Literary Echoes," *Books in Canada* 9, no. 3 (March 1980):8.

24. W. J. Keith, "The Case for Hugh Hood," *Canadian Forum,* October 1980, p. 28.

25. Kent Thompson, "Hugh Hood and His Expanding Universe," *Journal of Canadian Fiction* 3, no. 1 (Winter 1974):55.

26. Struthers, "An Interview with Hugh Hood," p. 38.

27. Geoff Hancock, "Hugh Hood's celebration of the millennium's end," *Quill & Quire,* November 1980, p. 40.

28. From Dante, Hood derives the notion of a divine comedy, and a salvific narrative. From Coleridge, he gets models of meditation and conversation in literature. Coleridge had the idea of "taking a very, very wide synthetic span and gradually allowing the connections to emerge" (*Before The Flood,* p. 63). Joyce, for Hood, is the "master of the dictionary" and "the master of the meanings of words" (*Before The Flood,* p. 64). Joyce's compilation of esoteric etymologies is what interests Hood, who thinks of himself as an encyclopedist and maker of catalogs. Then there are also Joyce's epiphanies, with which Hood makes a connection, for the epiphany as a "sudden flashing forth of intelligibility" (*Before The Flood,* p. 71) serves as a focal point for Hood's anagogical method. Like Proust, Hood sees our image-making faculty as a means both for grasping the world and for detaching ourselves from it. Hood is Proustian in his intellectual analysis of the nature of history and in his use of the metaphor of time. What Hood has learned from Anthony Powell has been techniques for moving around in a time span, looking at it "sometimes from the point of view of a man whose generation is coming to a close, but not in strict chronological order" (*Before The Flood,* p. 70). Hood is one with Powell in seeing society "as an infinite series of social relations" (*Before The Flood,* p. 69).

29. Sandler, "Near Proust And Yonge," p. 6.

30. Struthers, "An Interview with Hugh Hood," p. 61.

Chapter Two

1. William York Tindall, *The Literary Symbol* (Bloomington: Indiana University Press, 1955), p. 12.

2. Ibid.

3. W. Fowlie, "Symbolism, Literary," in *A New Catholic Encyclopedia* (New York: McGraw-Hill Book Co., 1967), 13:871.

4. A. J. M. Smith, ed., *The Canadian Century* (Toronto: Gage Educational Publishing, 1973), p. xviii.

5. I. M. Owen, "The Hood Line: Father, Son, and Holy Ghost," review of *None Genuine Without This Signature, Books in Canada,* August-September 1980, p. 10.

6. Frye, *Anatomy,* p. 54.

7. Ibid., p. 89.

8. "Hugh Hood and John Mills in Epistolary Conversation," *Fiddlehead,* no. 116 (Winter 1978), p. 145.

9. Struthers, "An Interview with Hugh Hood," p. 49.

10. John MacQueen, *Allegory (The Critical Idiom: 14)* (London: Methuen & Co., 1970), p. 1.

11. Ibid., p. 5.

12. Ibid., p. 18.

13. Erich Auerbach, *Mimesis: The Representation of Reality in Western Literature.* Trans. Willard Trask (New York: Doubleday Anchor Books, 1953), p. 229.

14. MacQueen, *Allegory,* p. 68.

15. Allen Tate, "The Symbolic Imagination," in *The Man of Letters in the Modern World* (New York: Meridian Books, 1955), p. 97.

16. Ibid., p. 112.

17. Hood, *Flying a Red Kite.* All quotations are from this edition and are denoted by *FRK* in the text.

18. "Hugh Hood and John Mills in Epistolary Conversation," p. 43.

19. Ibid., p. 137.

20. Struthers, "An Interview with Hugh Hood," p. 43.

21. Hugh Hood, *Around the Mountain: Scenes from Montreal Life* (Toronto, 1967). All quotations are from this edition and are denoted by *AM* in the text.

22. Struthers, "An Interview with Hugh Hood," p. 45.

23. Ibid., p. 44.

24. Ibid., p. 47.

25. Ibid., p. 52.

26. Hugh Hood, *The Fruit Man, The Meat Man & The Manager* (Ottawa, 1971). All quotations are from this edition and are denoted by *FM* within my text.

27. Struthers, "An Interview with Hugh Hood," p. 38.

28. E. M. Burke, "Grace," in *A New Catholic Encyclopedia,* 6:662.

29. Robert Lecker, "A Spirit of Communion: *The Swing in the Garden,*" in *Before The Flood,* p. 188.

30. Struthers, "An Interview with Hugh Hood," p. 41.

31. Patricia Morley, *The Comedians: Hugh Hood and Rudy Wiebe* (Toronto, 1977), p. 108.

32. New, "14: Fiction," p. 265.

33. Hugh Hood, *Dark Glasses* (Ottawa, 1976). All quotations are from this edition and are denoted by *DG* in the text.

34. Lawrence Mathews, "The Secular and the Sacral: Notes on *A New Athens* and Three Stories by Hugh Hood," in *Before The Flood*, p. 214.

35. Ibid., p. 220.

36. Ibid., p. 221.

37. Wayne Grady, "Fiction Chronicle," *Tamarack Review* 77–78 (Summer 1979):100.

38. Ibid.

39. Ibid., pp. 100–101.

40. Struthers, "An Interview with Hugh Hood," p. 32.

41. Ibid., pp. 32–33.

42. Ibid., p. 32.

43. Mathews, "Secular," p. 218.

44. Hugh Hood, *None Genuine Without This Signature* (Downsview, 1980). All quotations are from this edition and are denoted by *NG* in the text.

45. Hugh Hood, *Strength Down Centre: The Jean Béliveau Story* (Scarborough, Ontario, 1970). All quotations are from this edition are denoted by *SDC* within my text.

46. Robert Fulford, "An Interview with Hugh Hood," *Tamarack Review*, no. 66 (June 1975), p. 77.

Chapter Three

1. Hugh Hood, *White Figure, White Ground* (Toronto, 1964). All quotations are from this edition and are denoted by *WF* in the text.

2. Dennis Duffy, "Grace: The Novels of Hugh Hood," in *The Canadian Novel in the Twentieth Century*, ed. and introduction by George Woodcock (Toronto, 1975), p. 249.

3. Moss, *Sex and Violence*, p. 96.

4. Struthers, "An Interview with Hugh Hood," p. 57.

5. Ibid., p. 101.

6. Ibid., p. 23.

7. Ibid.

8. Ibid., p. 22.

9. Ibid., pp. 22–23.

10. Ibid., pp. 48–49.

11. Ibid., p. 41.

12. Ibid., p. 35.

13. Moss, *Sex and Violence*, pp. 97–100.

14. Struthers, "An Interview with Hugh Hood," p. 38.

15. Ibid., p. 59.

16. Desmond Pacey, review of *White Figure, White Ground, Fiddlehead*, no. 63 (Winter 1965), p. 71.

Chapter Four

1. Hugh Hood, *The Camera Always Lies* (New York, 1967). All quotations are from this edition and are denoted by *CAL* in the text.
2. Phyllis Grosskurth, "New Canadian Novels," *Saturday Night,* November 1967, p. 55.
3. Chris Redmond, "A Distorted Rehash of Real Life," *Queen's Journal,* 27 October 1967 (n.p.).
4. John Cowan, "Thoroughly Bad Novel," *Sherbrooke Daily Record,* 24 February 1968 (n.p.).
5. Robert Fulford, "Hugh Hood's misused talent," *Toronto Star,* 11 October 1967, p. 43.
6. J. E. Cirlot, *A Dictionary of Symbols,* trans. Jack Sage (New York: Philosophical Library, 1962), p. 144.
7. Struthers, "An Interview with Hugh Hood," p. 65.
8. Duffy, "Grace," p. 248.
9. Frye, *Anatomy,* p. 193.
10. Struthers, "An Interview with Hugh Hood," p. 65.
11. Frye, *Anatomy,* p. 186.

Chapter Five

1. Hugh Hood, *A Game of Touch* (Don Mills, Ontario, 1970). All quotations are from this edition and are denoted by *GT* in the text.
2. Morley, *The Comedians,* p. 39.
3. Ibid., pp. 42–43.
4. Hugh Hood and Seymour Segal, *Scoring: The Art of Hockey,* images by Seymour Segal; text by Hugh Hood (Ottawa, 1979), n.p.

Chapter Six

1. Hugh Hood, *You Cant Get There From Here* (Ottawa, 1972). All quotations are from this edition and are denoted by *YC* in the text.
2. Frye, *Anatomy,* p. 309.
3. Struthers, "An Interview with Hugh Hood," p. 58.
4. Morley, *The Comedians,* p. 50.
5. Struthers, "An Interview with Hugh Hood," p. 54.
6. Northrop Frye, *Fearful Symmetry* (Princeton: Princeton University Press, 1972), p. 135.
7. Ibid., p. 75.
8. Ibid., p. 135.
9. Joseph Jastrow, *Freud: His Dream and Sex Theories* (New York: Pocket Books Inc., 1955), p. 211.
10. Ibid.

11. Thomas More, *Utopia*, trans. and ed. H. V. S. Ogden (New York: Appleton-Century-Crofts, Inc., 1949), pp. 43–44.

Chapter Seven

1. Struthers, "An Interview with Hugh Hood," p. 61.
2. Ibid., p. 63.
3. Ibid., p. 61.
4. Hancock, "Hugh Hood's Celebration," p. 40.
5. Hugh Hood, letter to Naim Kattan, p. 15.
6. Struthers, "An Interview with Hugh Hood," p. 66.
7. "Hugh Hood and John Mills in Epistolary Conversation," p. 136.
8. Roland Barthes, *S/Z*, trans. Richard Miller (New York: Hill and Wang, 1974), p. 22.
9. Ibid., p. 68.
10. Hugh Hood, *The Swing in the Garden* (Ottawa, 1975). All quotations are from this edition and are denoted by *SG* in the text.
11. "Hugh Hood and John Mills in Epistolary Conversation," p. 135.
12. Fulford, "An Interview with Hugh Hood," p. 65.
13. Ibid., p. 77.
14. Keith Garebian, "At Home with the Hoods," *Montreal Star*, 19 November 1977, p. D-1.
15. John Mills, "The Blood Horse," review of *Close to the Sun Again* by Morley Callaghan; *The Doctor's Wife* by Brian Moore; and *A New Athens* by Hugh Hood, *Queen's Quarterly* 85 (Spring 1978):64.
16. Lecker, "Spirit," p. 200.
17. Frank Kermode, ed., *English Pastoral Poetry* (From the Beginnings to Marvell) (New York: W. W. Norton & Co., 1972), p. 14.
18. Lecker, "Spirit," pp. 187–210.
19. Ibid., p. 191.
20. Ibid., p. 194.
21. Laurence Lerner, *The Uses of Nostalgia* (New York: Schocken Books, 1972), p. 103.
22. William Empson, *Some Versions of Pastoral* (Harmondsworth: Penguin Books, 1966), p. 13.
23. Lecker, "Spirit," p. 197.
24. Letter by Hugh Hood to Keith Garebian, 30 April 1980.
25. "Hugh Hood and John Mills in Epistolary Conversation," p. 137.
26. Fulford, "An Interview with Hugh Hood," p. 68.
27. R. W. B. Lewis, *The American Adam* (Chicago: The University of Chicago Press, 1966), p. 5.
28. Ibid., pp. 20–21.
29. Ibid., p. 41.

30. Hugh Hood, *A New Athens* (Ottawa, 1977). All quotations are from this edition and are denoted by *NA* in the text.

31. Struthers, "An Interview with Hugh Hood," p. 80.

32. John Mills, "Hugh Hood and the Anagogical Method," in *Before The Flood*, p. 104.

33. Struthers, "An Interview with Hugh Hood," p. 71.

34. Mills, "Hugh Hood and the Anagogical Method," p. 97.

35. Struthers, "An Interview with Hugh Hood," p. 31.

36. Mills, "Hugh Hood and the Anagogical Method," pp. 106–7.

37. A. M. Klein, *The Second Scroll* (Toronto: McClelland and Stewart Ltd., 1966), pp. 103–13.

38. Hugh Hood, *Reservoir Ravine* (Ottawa, 1979). All quotations are from this edition and are denoted by *RR* in the text.

39. J. S. Woodsworth, "Mobilizing Progressive Opinion in Canada," in *Forum (Canadian Life and Letters 1920–70)*, ed. J. L. Granatstein and Peter Stevens (Toronto: University of Toronto Press, 1972), pp. 28–29.

40. William Blake, "The Marriage of Heaven and Hell," in *The Complete Writings Of William Blake*, ed. Geoffrey Keynes (London: Oxford University Press, 1966), p. 151.

41. Hood and his family lived for many years in a Montreal parish named after St. Raphael. His mother died in a nursing home dedicated to St. Raphael. His elder daughter is named Sarah. Such are the intersections of biblical myth, autobiography, and fiction.

Chapter Eight

1. George Lukács, *The Theory of the Novel*, trans. Anna Bostock (Cambridge, Mass.: MIT Press, 1971), p. 71.

2. Paul Ricoeur, *The Symbolism of Evil*, trans. Emerson Buchanan (Boston: Beacon Press, 1969), pp. 72–73.

3. Ernest Becker, *The Structure of Evil* (New York: Free Press, 1968), pp. 235–36.

4. Ibid., p. 172.

5. Lukács, *Theory of the Novel*, p. 78.

Selected Bibliography

All of Hood's books are named under primary sources; but only selected items are named under secondary sources. Within the first section items appear chronologically according to the date of publication.

PRIMARY SOURCES

"Theories of Imagination in English Thinkers 1650–1790." Diss., University of Toronto, 1955.

Flying a Red Kite. Toronto: Ryerson Press, 1962.

White Figure, White Ground. Toronto: Ryerson Press, 1964.

Around the Mountain: Scenes from Montreal Life. Toronto: Peter Martin Associates, 1967.

The Camera Always Lies. New York: Harcourt, Brace & World, 1967.

A Game of Touch. Don Mills, Ontario: Longman Canada, 1970.

Strength Down Centre: The Jean Béliveau Story. Scarborough, Ontario: Prentice-Hall of Canada, 1970.

The Fruit Man, The Meat Man & The Manager. Ottawa: Oberon Press, 1971.

You Cant Get There From Here. Ottawa: Oberon Press, 1972.

The Governor's Bridge Is Closed. Ottawa: Oberon Press, 1973.

The Swing in the Garden. Part One of *The New Age/Le Nouveau Siècle.* Ottawa: Oberon Press, 1975.

Dark Glasses. Ottawa: Oberon Press, 1976.

A New Athens. Part Two of *The New Age/Le Nouveau Siècle.* Ottawa: Oberon Press, 1977.

Selected Stories. Ottawa: Oberon Press, 1978.

Reservoir Ravine. Part Three of *The New Age/Le Nouveau Siècle.* Ottawa: Oberon Press, 1979.

Scoring: The Art of Hockey. Images by Seymour Segal; Text by Hugh Hood. Ottawa: Oberon Press, 1979.

None Genuine Without This Signature. Downsview, Ontario: ECW Press, 1980.

SECONDARY SOURCES

Cameron, Barry. Review of *Dark Glasses. Fiddlehead,* no. 115 (Fall 1977), pp. 145–47. Highly favorable. Illuminating textual criticism of "Thanksgiving: Between Junetown and Caintown."

Cloutier, Pierre. "All in All in Africa." *Books in Canada,* November/December 1972, pp. 26–27. Most of Hood's work has been an allegory of salvation, and *You Cant Get There From Here* "measures the gap separating the human from the divine . . . and brings the Canadian novel very close to sacred text."

Duffy, Dennis. "A New Athens, The New Jerusalem, A New Atlantis." *Fiddlehead,* no. 117 (Spring 1978), pp. 101–108. Favorable review of *A New Athens,* but faults Hood for often passing off ideas as feelings.

———. "A Quiet Rage. Too Sane to Get at the Vertigo of Our Times." *Globe and Mail,* 16 September 1972, Sec. Entertainment-Travel, p. 31. *You Cant Get There From Here* says a lot about Canada, but the novel is too sane and too level-headed.

———. "Grace: The Novels of Hugh Hood." In: *The Canadian Novel in the Twentieth Century.* Edited and introduction by George Woodcock. Toronto: McClelland and Stewart, 1975, pp. 242–57. Deals chiefly with the first three novels, and argues that "balancing between a sense of the real and a glimpse of the visionary, they bring to us a picture of this world and the grace that is there for anyone who would reach out for it."

Foster, Malcolm. "A Delightful Collection of Stories." *Gazette* (Montreal), 23 October 1971, Sec. 4, p. 46. Hood's characters in *The Fruit Man, The Meat Man & The Manager* live far better than the characters in his novels.

French, William. "Scrambled Scrimmage, Fumbled Ball." *Globe Magazine,* 24 October 1970, p. 36. Finds *A Game of Touch* confused. "There are some good moments, but they are rare (but what could you expect from a novel featuring federal-provincial relations?)."

Fulford, Robert. "An Interview with Hugh Hood." *Tamarack Review,* no. 66 (June 1975), pp. 65–77. Hood discusses his New Age project, prior to the publication of *The Swing in the Garden,* and uses the term "documentary fantasy" to describe his epical fiction.

———. "Hugh Hood—a Writer Whose Ambition Is Limitless." *Toronto Star,* 27 October 1973, Sec. G, p. 5. Favorable review of *The Governor's Bridge Is Closed.* "In a world of mourners, he's a celebrant. In a world fragmented, he reaches for wholeness."

———. "Hugh Hood's Misused Talent." Review of *The Camera Always Lies* and *Around the Mountain. Toronto Star,* 11 October 1967, p. 43. Fulford invents the canard that Hood is a superior journalist and an inferior novelist.

Garebian, Keith. "*The Swing in the Garden:* Hugh Hood's Pastoral." Unpublished paper delivered at "The Commonwealth in Canada" conference at Concordia University on 19 October 1978. Determines the pastoral form in a Canadian "blameworthy After-The-Fall style that does not, however, shrink from new tensions that provoke our conventional understanding of relationships between the new and the old, the individual and society, man and God, knowledge and innocence."

Godfrey, Dave. "Turning New Leaves (2)." *Canadian Forum* 42 (January 1963: 229–30. Generally favorable review of *Flying a Red Kite.*

Hancock, Geoff. "Hugh Hood's Celebration of the Millenium's End." *Quill & Quire,* November 1980, p. 40. Hood explains that he does not like the "artificiality" of the dramatic forms of art. He does not see suffering as a means to redemption, for he feels that life is already saved. His characters are really portraits of "Canadian ranges of behaviour" or "Canadian moral possibilities."

"Hugh Hood and John Mills in Epistolary Conversation." *Fiddlehead,* no. 116 (Winter 1978), pp. 133–46. A prickly, witty, tendentious, and candid correspondence about the aesthetics of fiction. A result of Mills's unfavorable review of *The Swing in the Garden.* Hood explains his allegorical framework and literary principles.

Keith, W. J. "The Case for Hugh Hood." *Canadian Forum,* October 1980, pp. 27–29. Highly favorable review of *None Genuine Without This Signature.* Finds "precision of detail, delicacy of nuance, firmness of (albeit inconspicuous) structure, a smooth felicity of language, and warmly human compassion."

Mills, John. Review of *The Swing in the Garden;* and *Two Stories: The Drubbing of Nesterenko & First Loves* by Hanford Woods. *Fiddlehead,* no. 112 (Winter 1977), pp. 143–46. Finds the book formless and without a story in the conventional sense. Hood's bland Catholic optimism verges on Pelagianism and results in the vision of a Norman Rockwell.

Morley, Patricia. *The Comedians: Hugh Hood & Rudy Wiebe.* Toronto: Clarke, Irwin & Co., 1977. Uses Northrop Frye's definition of comic narrative to examine the fiction of Hood and Wiebe. Covers Hood only till *The Swing in the Garden.*

Moss, John. *Sex and Violence in the Canadian Novel: The Ancestral Present.* Toronto: McClelland and Stewart, 1977. Comments at length on *White Figure, White Ground* to show how Hood delves into the sexual possibilities of the Urthona triangle.

Sandler, Linda. "Near Proust and Yonge: That's Where Hugh Hood Grew Up and Why He's Making a 12-Novel Bid for Immortality." *Books in Canada,* December 1975, pp. 5–7. "Hood is not so much a novelist as an inspired social historian. . . . Hood's mind is always travelling from an elevated metaphysical plane, through an esoteric literary one, down to the very solid soil. And the reverse."

Solecki, Sam. "Metafiction or Metahistory?" *Canadian Forum,* December-January 1977, pp. 37–38. Calls *A New Athens* "disconcertingly undramatic, at times even unfictive." Questions Matt's "almost static view" of Ontario history.

Stratford, Philip. "The Artist's Life." *Saturday Night,* October 1964, p. 30. *White Figure, White Ground* is a story of "white on white, not one of marked contrasts and moral chaos, but one of subtle and satisfying variations within the limitations of the normal and the possible."

Struthers, J. R. (Tim), ed. *Before The Flood.* Downsview: ECW Press, 1979. Excellent anthology of criticism and features. Contains an introductory essay by Hood on his earliest tastes in reading, and Struthers's long, highly informative and engaging interview with Hood. John Mills discusses Hood's anagogical method; John Orange writes of Hood's place in Canadian fiction; Dennis Duffy looks closely at two short stories to investigate what happens in the writing; Patrick Blandford examines bicultural tensions; George Woodcock notes the relationship between power and order; Robert Lecker writes comprehensively on the spirit of communion in *The Swing in the Garden;* and Lawrence Mathews looks at the secular and the sacral in *A New Athens* and three short stories. Includes an extensive bibliography compiled by Struthers.

Thompson, Kent. "Hugh Hood and His Expanding Universe." *Journal of Canadian Fiction* 3, no. 1 (Winter 1974): 55–59. Hood is very interested in relativity, which means that his characters "generally lead lives of confused human ignorance in a universe of time and space." This universe is continually expanding as each person and event help it to do so.

Woodcock, George. "Ancestral Voices." *Books in Canada,* February 1976, pp. 3–7. Surveys Canadian Literature's fascination with the 1930s, and evaluates *The Swing in the Garden,* saying it is "on a level nearer to Jules Romain than to the master of the Faubourg St. Germain." However, Hood's evocation of Toronto is called astonishing.

Index